JONATHAN SWIFT
Poems selected by DEREK MAHON

JONATHAN SWIFT

Poems selected by DEREK MAHON

faber and faber

This selection first published in 2001
by Faber and Faber Ltd
3 Queen Square London WC1N 3AU

Photoset by Parker Typesetting Service, Leicester
Printed in Italy

A CIP record for this book
is available from the British Library
ISBN 0—571— 20715—4

10 9 8 7 6 5 4 3 2 1

Contents

Introduction

If the facts are recalcitrant, what of the legend? Even now a myth persists about Swift's 'madness', as if no sane person could take such a dim view of human nature. Which means that even now he is relevant – perhaps especially now, when so many features of the Age of Reason are again discernible, not to say obtrusive: strident economic 'growth', a mechanistic model of the universe, a constant expectation of imminent 'chaos'. The madness rumour started in his lifetime and achieved specious authority at the hands of later writers who deplored his alleged misanthropy – a term he himself used to mean 'philosophical pessimism'. It's now recognized that Swift's problems were physiological in origin. The madness theory has been discredited, yet its spectral residue may have contributed to an interesting recent development, the rediscovery of Swift the poet. Widely perceived as a sort of anti-poet and critically disregarded for two centuries as offering nothing very dense or visionary to the scholarly mind or the inquiring spirit, he has since been read anew as one of the great eccentrics; for, despite his aspiration to a tough-minded detachment, there is great emotion in his work, great turmoil under the hard, glittering surface. Admirers of Augustan elegance and post-modern 'cool' will find him a remarkably hot-headed figure, a flamboyant character as colourful in his way as Wilde or Yeats; indeed the personality goes far towards explaining the continuing fascination of his verse which, unlike the prose satires, presented a recurrent means of dramatic self-projection. The enigmatic persona thus created, austere yet kindly – that of the 'Dean', the 'Drapier', 'Dr Swift' – spoke with a distinctive Anglo-Irish voice, liberal, witty and vertiginously ironical, whose echo is still audible even now.

The complete poems run to several hundred pages. Of those in this selection only 'A Description of the Morning' and 'A Description of a City Shower' were published before his appointment to the deanery of St. Patrick's Cathedral, Dublin, in 1713, at the age of forty-six. *Gulliver's Travels*, and the bulk of the verse, were written after this date – in Ireland, for the most part, though often with an English readership in mind. We are to picture a solitary though gregarious middle-aged bachelor of medium height, notable for piercing blue eyes and a formidable asperity of manner, alternately jocular and despondent, who passes his leisure hours with a circle of devoted admirers, male and female; who walks and rides a great deal; and who spends too much time alone, morosely contemplating the Hanoverian succession, the triumph of Whiggery and his own exile from the ministerial ambience where he once shone. Dublin is his native city and he has mixed feelings about it. There are two principal women in his life, Esther Johnson and Esther Vanhomrigh. The former, 'Stella', is a neighbour and frequent visitor, one of his inner circle, indeed his oldest friend; the latter, 'Vanessa', twenty years his junior, lives importunately in lodgings and in her house at Celbridge on the river Liffey, twelve miles from town. Good girl, bad girl – though Vanessa, of course, was a good girl too. Edgily aware of each other, these women provide the emotional stimulus and consolation in a seemingly sardonic, and often splenetic, existence. Other friends include Thomas Sheridan, schoolmaster and grandfather of the playwright, who has a property at Quilca, Co. Cavan, and the Achesons of Markethill, Co. Armagh, where he is a frequent guest. The parish of Laracor, near Trim, a living he retained to the end of his days, where he built his own house and planted willows, provides peace and quiet, when required, among the thoughtful horses of Co. Meath.

Gulliver remarks of the Houyhnhnms: 'In poetry they must be allowed to excel all other mortals; wherein the justice of their similes, and the minuteness, as well as the exactness of their descriptions, are indeed inimitable.' Of the Laputans he says: 'Imagination, fancy and invention, they are wholly strangers to, nor have any words in their language by which those ideas can be expressed.' The first of these observations we might take to refer to Swift's friends Pope and Gay, authors respectively of *The Rape of the Lock* and *The Beggar's Opera*; and indeed to Swift himself. The second is more problematical; the creator of Lilliput and Brobding-nag has never been thought to lack fancy and invention, but Swift the poet has often been thought wanting in 'imagina-tion'. If we mean imagination in the Coleridgean sense, this is fair enough. There is not much of Shakespeare in him, though there is something of Dr John Donne, Dean of St Paul's. Other precursors usually noted include Milton's 'Il Penseroso', whose octosyllabic couplet he adopted; the first Samuel Butler, author of *Hudibras*, whose comic rhymes he imitated and surpassed; and Rochester, whose aphoristic vituperation provided a bracing model of plain speech.

Swift's directness and clarity of image, his unmediated transparency and colloquial vigour, have given rise to a situation where, seemingly yielding little to close analysis, he suffers or perhaps enjoys critical neglect but knows, like Burns, popular immortality, especially in Ireland. Traces of his mystique are scattered throughout the culture. Nor is this attributable solely to *Gulliver*. There is a folk memory of the generously seditious *Drapier's Letters*; but it's remembered, above all, that he made provision in his will for a lunatic asylum which, established in due course as the prestigious St Patrick's Hospital, continues to thrive:

> He gave the little Wealth he had,
> To build a House for Fools and Mad:
> And shew'd by one satyric Touch,
> No Nation wanted it so much:
> That Kingdom he hath left his Debtor,
> I wish it soon may have a Better.

All his verse is in the strict sense occasional – in his own perhaps disingenuous words, 'trifles never intended for publick view'. Like Byron later, he wrote not as an artist but as a gentleman amateur, or so he liked to imply. The poems, technically simple but rhetorically complex, owe much of their effect to the known character of the author and his contemporary celebrity.

Eliot once rebuked 'those who condemn or ignore *en bloc* the poetry of the eighteenth century on the ground that it is "prosaic"' when most of it is 'not prosaic enough'. Swift, in theory and practice, is one of the great 'prosaic' poets. Dryden advised him in youth that he would 'never be a poet'; but this prediction was based on early exercises like 'Ode to the King' (William III), where the young practitioner still aspired to some version of the sublime. The mature poet, the Swift we think we know, took no interest in the sublime except as an object of derision. The author of trifles, *écrivant* rather than *écrivain*, amused scribbler rather than dedicated artist (or so he would have us believe), he set out his view of poetic vocation in the scurrilous rap 'On Poetry: A Rapsody', that the whole thing, in the circumstances pertaining, is a lot of trivial nonsense, in Grub Street or at Court; yet, given the intolerable, self-pleasing cant of the age, he found it hard, like Juvenal, 'not to write satire'. But if he was quick to recognize the ridiculous in the sublime, the idiotic in the heroic, he shared (and took very seriously) the low-level anxiety of his time in regard to 'chaos', whose 'dread empire' Pope evoked in *The Dunciad*. With Swift this was not only a cultural but a personal fear. Any lapse from a briskly rational standard, in sexual matters for instance, and Pandora's box might turn into a temple of the winds.

Owing perhaps to their genial tone, none of the poems were more popular in his lifetime than the two 'Descriptions' with which this selection opens. Appearing first in *The Tatler* in 1709 and 1710 respectively, the 'Morning' and the 'Shower' established this Irish provincial as a poet of London, a thing of great importance to him then and later. The first, said Steele, introducing the poem, was 'not only a description of the morning but of the morning in town, nay, of the morning at this end of town, where my kinsman at present lodges' (i.e., the West End); and we notice at once a characteristic attention to detail. This is both loving and quizzical as he introduces a theme more fully developed later, that of dirt and waste disposal, already associated with sexuality:

Now *Betty* from her Masters bed had flown,
And softly stole to discompose her own.
The Slipshod Prentice from his Masters Door,
Had par'd the Dirt, and Sprinkled round the Floor.

A townsman, urban if not always urbane, Swift delighted in the noise and squalor of city life, the 'dialogical polyphony' in Bakhtinian phrase (a delight still evident as late as 'Verses made for Women who cry Apples, &c.'): whatever about misanthropy and perceptual problems, he lent an appreciative ear, eye and nose (nose especially) to the physical facts of the world he knew. The tone is not satirical but tolerant, humorous, even enchanted. The dynamics of order and disorder are uninflected by anxiety or stricture; the unusual pentameter (later discarded) imposes a deadpan formality; the chaos control is barely perceptible. If, as has been said, dirt is matter in the wrong place, Swift's 'proper words in proper places' is a principle of stylistic hygiene. 'Not cold but intense' is how Geoffrey Hill describes Swift's mode of perception, noting particularly a capacity 'to transform, say, autocratic disdain into a cherishing particularity', and the ambiguity of his attitude to the anarchic: 'In principle he abhorred all its aspects; poetically he reacted to it with a kindling of creative delight.' Autocratic disdain, though, was never a Swiftian mode; he never sneered at the generality of 'folks'. Quite the contrary: fair liberty was all his cry.

As a poet he was a late starter, but the 'Shower' was an immediate hit: 'the best thing I ever writ; there never was such a shower since Danaë's'. Parodically derived from all previous literary floods – *Genesis*, Ovid – and sharing the social alertness of Pope and Gay (it was Swift who first suggested the idea of *The Beggar's Opera*), the 'Shower' overflows with a love of London and a love of life, even or perhaps especially in the boisterous final triplet designed to mock the Drydenesque pomposity of triplets. At this stage he went with the flow of the age, a time of rapid population growth and expanding newspaper readership – an inflationary age, like ours, of financial speculation, sophisticated philistinism and harsh comedy, when Hobbes's version of the 'selfish gene' promoted a culture of winners and losers, the club and the street. These mock-pastoral genre pieces, like most of Swift, are best read with an eye to historical context, especially visual context. Brisk Susan and the Beau in his sedan chair, clothes and objects, the furniture of room and thoroughfare, create a theatrical space which has become, with time, almost the substantive content of the verse. Like Hogarth he is a narrative painter of the period, rich in material fact and vivid detail; he has inscribed, engraved even, certain aspects of early eighteenth-century experience indelibly on the historical memory, and not only the more scabrous and grotesque. His genuine interest in life below stairs, for example (see 'Mary the Cook-maid's Letter'), is in the same spirit as Hogarth's later group portrait of his own domestic servants.

'Cadenus and Vanessa', the title echoing Shakespeare's 'Venus and Adonis', its length and ingenuity testifying to the vitality of this relationship, was first drafted about 1713, shortly before his Dublin appointment. Inhabiting a theatrical space of the period, the erotic school-room, it's a closet Restoration comedy of manners, mistaken motives and sexual innuendo, owing much to his fellow Dublin graduates Congreve and Farquhar (also to Molière), its manipulative showmanship barely concealed by the baroque machinery. There was scandal on its unauthorized publication; a certain caddishness was deplored. Swift's friend Patrick Delany spoke sadly of the 'idle vanity' of 'these vile verses':

But what Success *Vanessa* met
Is to the World a Secret yet:
Whether the Nymph, to please her Swain,
Talks in a high Romantick Strain;
Or whether he at last descends
To like with less Seraphick Ends;
Or, to compound the Business, whether
They temper Love and Books together;
Must never to Mankind be told,
Nor shall the conscious Muse unfold.

'So bright a nymph to come unsought', the ingenue Vanessa, like Stella herself, was the talk of the town then and later; the story fairly crackles with sexuality. Vanessa followed him to Ireland against his wishes; endured isolation and neglect; died young, and left her property not to Swift but to Swift's friend the philosopher George Berkeley, Bishop of Cloyne, whom she hardly knew.

Stella, whose tutor he had been in the early days at Moor Park, Surrey, first appeared under that name (borrowed from Sidney) in the series of birthday poems he wrote for her in Ireland, starting when she was thirty-eight and he forty-six. A potent mixture of gallantry and naturalism, these lyrical exercises, consciously anti-idealistic yet equidistant from the cynical seduction verse of the previous century, recall the amorous ratiocination of Donne, the assumption being one of mutual equality and back-chat, 'sense and wit'. It was Swift's opinion that modern love was a fraud based on unrealities at once grandiose and sordid, whereas he and Stella had achieved a complex, unillusioned relation founded on intimacy of mind as much as body. Goldsmith praised his 'boldness'; and Robert Graves, writing about what he calls the Age of Obsequiousness, remarks that among the poets of the period 'the only personal Muse I can recall is Swift's Stella.' Swift was unusual in this as in so much else, and the warmth and realism, fresh insight and startling candour of these extraordinary love poems make them unique for their time. 'Not the gravest of divines', he specializes in what he called 'raillery', the teasing familiarity and back-handed compliment he established, unilaterally and no doubt a little tiresomely, as their private language; but regular 'lapses' into plangency and charm, as in the delightful 'Stella at Woodpark', or the turbulent stoicism of the last birthday poem (1727), give the emotional game away:

> O then, whatever Heav'n intends,
> Take Pity on your pitying Friends:
> Nor let your Ills affect your Mind,
> To fancy they can be unkind.
> Me, surely me, you ought to spare,
> Who gladly would your Suff'rings share;
> Or give my Scrap of Life to you,
> And think it far beneath your Due;
> You, to whose Care so oft I owe,
> That I'm alive to tell you so.

Not too much need be made, at this stage, of the scatological poems, few in number, written in the period of disorientation following Stella's death; they might even be ascribed, paradoxically, to the good influence of her living presence, now withdrawn. Celia and Corinna are the unfortunate whipping-girls of Swift's bereavement and despair; the rage is cosmic, the sadism a kind of blasphemy. Irvin Ehrenpreis speaks of 'the comedy of sexual prosthesis' and points out that the voyeuristic boudoir visit and discovery of cosmetic aids were practically a topos of the period, with a literary genealogy going back, once again, to Ovid. The satirist isn't getting at the girls, he suggests, much less the female economy as such, but at the vanity fair of high society, 'the social imposition of a preconceived sexual idealism' and, in Swift's phrase, 'that ridiculous passion which hath no being but in play-books and romances'. W. J. McCormack sees his 'excesses' and 'obsessions' in this regard as less a 'biographical oddity' than a 'cultural symptom'; and Victoria Glendinning, while reproving Swift's 'peculiar and impertinent treatment of women', charitably interprets the scatological writings, in psychiatric terms, as analytical 'work' on 'a universal neurosis'. Everything in historical context, everything 'situational'; anachronistic modern attitudes won't help us here:

> Thus finishing his grand Survey,
> The Swain disgusted slunk away,
> Repeating in his amorous Fits:
> 'Oh! *Celia, Celia, Celia* shits!'

The second couplet, delicately omitted by George Faulkner from his 1735 edition of the poems, and even by Herbert Davis from his old-spelling 1967 edition of the *Poetical Works*, on which this selection is based, has its comical and unpathological equivalent in *Directions to Servants*, where Swift advises the Chamber Maid as follows: 'Do not carry down the necessary Vessels for the Fellows to see, but empty them out of the Window, for your Lady's Credit. It is highly improper for Men Servants to know that fine Ladies have Occasion for such Utensils.' The misfortunes of Celia and Corinna must be balanced not only by the Stella poems but by Swift's more characteristic relishing of the physical, and his benign influence on the circle of strong-minded, witty women, poets among them, who were a constant presence in his Dublin life: Mary Barber, Constantia Grierson, Laetitia Pilkington. To Mary Delany, while praising her eyes, he complains of 'a pernicious heresy . . . that it is the duty of your sex to be fools in every article except what is merely domestic'. He was, in his own fashion, a ladies' man – a fact noticed by the exuberant heroine of Erica Jong's *Fanny* (1980), who hits it off with him: '. . . a curious fellow, the cleverest man I e'er had met . . . and, I believe, much misunderstood.' There's a certain breezy, play-acting misogyny sometimes but, unlike most of his contemporaries, he takes women seriously, and the complexity of his attitude merely reflects the actual complexity of real-life gender relations.

The Anglo-Ireland to which he returned in 1714, after the death of Queen Anne and the fall of the Tories, was a rackety place. Roy Foster speaks of its 'gamey flavour' and 'ruthless but ironic pursuit of style'; the words 'savagery' and 'ferocity' also occur. Protestant hegemony was absolute, the majority legislated into subjection while 'civil' society toasted 'the glorious, pious and immortal memory of the great and good King William, who redeemed us from popery, slavery, arbitrary power, brass money and wooden shoes'. Swift, out of favour with government and suspected of Jacobitism, cut a solitary figure in this ripe milieu, though by no means an invisible one. No one was ever invisible in Dublin, which encourages the performative instinct: see and be seen. The psychology of Berkeley's *New Theory of Vision* (1709), and his later notion that 'to be is to be perceived', must have owed something to these conditions. Both within and beyond his chosen coterie Swift was a cynosure at all times, incorporating this as an imaginative principle into the work. He lived in an age of insectology and optical science, but had no need of Gulliver's spectacles and pocket telescope, or of Celia's magnifying glass, to tell him he occupied a *camera obscura*; even his introspection was extroverted: 'When a true genius appears in the world you may know him by this sign, that the dunces are all in confederacy against him.' Paranoia perhaps – though, as Delmore Schwartz observed, paranoia can be justified. Politically marginalized, his correspondence opened for evidence of sedition, he had good reason to think himself persecuted:

> Had he but spar'd his Tongue and Pen,
> He might have rose like other Men.

He inhabited a social and linguistic ghetto, albeit a privileged one. Beyond the English 'pale', and even within it, lay the alternative, indeed the original 'native Irish' culture, largely invisible to the urban eye; though Dublin itself was a bilingual city, with Irish-speaking poets in residence. Swift would have known no Irish, or a *cúpla focal* at most, but something of the Gaelic spirit got through to him. Through Sheridan he met the great, blind composer Carolan, who is said to have played the harp in the deanery. Tradition attributes to Carolan the air and the English version of Hugh MacGowran's 'Pléaráca na Ruarcach' ('O'Rourke's Revel') on which Swift based 'The Description of an Irish Feast'. He had an affinity with the Gaelic poets, particularly in the vehemence of his satire. It may not be entirely fanciful to trace an analogy between his own extremity and that of Gaeldom's great elegist, his near-contemporary Eoghan Ó Rathaille (1675–1729); and, sure enough, folklore records or imagines a spirited encounter between the Dean and the Kerry poet in the summer of 1723, when Swift toured Munster.

His gift to subsequent Irish writers (to speak only of Ireland) has been immense. With him the principal themes are already in place: 'race' and religion, cabin and Big House, famine and genocide, internal exile, sexual inhibition, the language question, and a complicated attitude towards the imperial neighbour. Representations of the body in Joyce and Beckett owe much to him, as does the 'savage indignation' of Yeats and Kavanagh. Beckett's taxonomy of laughter in *Watt* is decidedly Swiftian; somewhere behind it lie the ontological predicament of the Yahoos and the scrupulous grotesquerie of *A Modest Proposal*. Beckett identifies three laughs, all known to Swift, the bitter, the hollow and the mirthless: 'The bitter laugh laughs at that which is not good, it is the ethical laugh. The hollow laugh laughs at that which is not true, it is the intellectual laugh. Not good! Not true! Well well. But the mirthless laugh . . . is the laugh of laughs, the *risus purus*, the laugh laughing at the laugh, the beholding, the saluting of the highest joke, in a word the laugh that laughs – silence please – at that which is unhappy.' Swift laughed bitterly and hollowly at the misgovernment of Ireland, of England indeed, and mirthlessly at his (and our) existential situation. As for his satirical panache, we can look back on it now with nostalgia; for, as Adorno pointed out, the mode has been made redundant. How do you satirize achieved nihilism or an absolute consensus?

Anxiously awaiting the mail-boat at Holyhead in 1727, after his last visit to England, he wrote:

> I never was in hast before
> To reach that slavish hateful shore
> Before, I always found the wind
> To me was most malicious kind.

He railed often enough against the 'slavish hateful shore', the 'land of slaves' where he was obliged to live and where he expected to die 'like a poisoned rat in a hole', while privately conceding that 'in truth, I have no discontent at living here'. If a sense of grievance at his relegation to a fine house in a convivial capital full of friends and admirers seems exaggerated, it must be understood as a literary device. The air of life-sentence he cultivated aligned him imaginatively with the disempowered and persecuted, and placed him at a creatively useful distance from the centre of power; yet he looked constantly to London, the scene of his conspicuous early years, where the larger reputations were made. Despite his audacity and hauteur, reputation mattered greatly to him; and his best-known poem, 'Verses on the Death of Dr Swift', written in the 1730s during his sixties and intended for posthumous publication, was a bid to pre-empt and control how he would be seen by posterity. A bid which didn't wholly fail: he is often taken at his word, and the 'impartial' panegyric constituting the final section accepted as simple fact. Aside from its biographical interest we can now see that the distinction of the poem lies in its remarkable technique, its pro-active grasp and embodiment of gossip and transience: Swift's voice is only one among many, albeit one aiming for the last word. 'History is gossip', says Gore Vidal, also guilty of 'the sin of wit', and Swift's poems are full of gossip, his own and others'; they throng with people and voices, so that the private play takes place in the theatre of the world:

My female Friends, whose tender Hearts
Have better learn'd to act their Parts,
Receive the News in *doleful Dumps*,
'The Dean is dead, (*and what is Trumps?*).'

Swift's is a Rabelaisian and a Brechtian world, a thieves' kitchen, a site of vice and predation embracing pickpockets and politicians, Gin Lane and the Court of St James's. His nausea, vertigo and 'excremental vision', synecdoche of the body politic, compare with those of Baudelaire, yet he has something Baudelaire lacks, a vernacular zest (see, for example, 'Tom Clinch'); far from being a misanthrope in the usual sense, he revelled in life's feast. Street cries, music to his ears till he grew deaf, echo throughout. He had a ludic taste for popular forms and idioms; indeed, the only noticeable 'development' in technique, once he gets into his stride, is the adoption of an ever more racy, conversational style often incorporating 'Irish' rhymes and turns of phrase. Folk-song he preferred to Italian opera, street ballads to Handel and Purcell (parodied in 'A Cantata'). At his best, as in this selection (the choice makes itself), he is a light, fast, indeed *swift* poet, again like Byron, riding helter-skelter a current of kinetic energy with streamlined fluency. The virtuosity is extraordinary – though, strangely, the magical or visionary vein is reserved for the science fiction and invisible cities of *Gulliver*. 'On Dreams', for example, is strictly deterministic.

No one, said Hazlitt, had written 'so many lack-a-daisical, slip-shod, tedious, trifling, foolish, fantastical verses as he, which are so little an imputation on the wisdom of the writer; and which, in fact, only shew his readiness to oblige others, and to forget himself.' This aleatoric aspect of his poetic practice extends to the publishing history, which is a shambles of confusing devices including anonymous and involuntary publication, variant texts and disputed authorship. The poems seem to offer themselves as provisional drafts rather than finished compositions. Often we are dealing with a joint project, as with Stella who 'collected' and perhaps co-wrote some of the poems, or with one part of a co-operative venture involving Delany, Sheridan or Anne Acheson. Audience participation is encouraged; referred attitudes and attributed opinions are everywhere, friendly or hostile responses anticipated. Eminently situational, Swift is a gift to reception theory. How we read him now depends very largely on our own response to a singular personality and the enduring psychodrama he so graphically projects.

Derek Mahon

JONATHAN SWIFT

A Description of the Morning
The Tatler, Numb. 9. From Thursday April 28.
to Saturday April 30. 1709

Now hardly here and there a Hackney-Coach
Appearing, show'd the Ruddy Morns Approach.
Now *Betty* from her Masters Bed had flown,
And softly stole to discompose her own.
The Slipshod Prentice from his Masters Door,
Had par'd the Dirt, and Sprinkled round the Floor.
Now *Moll* had whirl'd her Mop with dext'rous Airs,
Prepar'd to Scrub the Entry and the Stairs.
The Youth with Broomy Stumps began to trace
The Kennel-Edge, where Wheels had worn the Place.
The Smallcoal-Man was heard with Cadence deep,
'Till drown'd in Shriller Notes of *Chimney-Sweep.*
Duns at his Lordships Gate began to meet,
And Brickdust *Moll* had Scream'd through half a Street.
The Turnkey now his Flock returning sees,
Duly let out a Nights to Steal for Fees.
The watchful Bailiffs take their silent Stands,
And School-Boys lag with Satchels in their Hands.

A Description of a City Shower

The Tatler, Numb. 238. From Saturday October 14.
to Tuesday October 17. 1710.

Careful Observers may fortel the Hour
(By sure Prognosticks) when to dread a Show'r:
While Rain depends, the pensive Cat gives o'er
Her Frolicks, and pursues her Tail no more.
Returning Home at Night, you'll find the Sink
Strike your offended Sense with double Stink.
If you be wise, then go not far to Dine,
You spend in Coach-hire more than save in Wine,
A coming Show'r your shooting Corns presage,
Old Aches throb, your hollow Tooth will rage.
Sauntring in Coffee-house is *Dulman* seen;
He damns the Climate, and complains of Spleen.

    Mean while the South rising with dabbled Wings,
A Sable Cloud a-thwart the Welkin flings,
That swill'd more Liquor than it could contain,
And like a Drunkard gives it up again.
Brisk *Susan* whips her Linen from the Rope,
While the first drizzling Show'r is born aslope,
Such is that Sprinkling which some careless Quean
Flirts on you from her Mop, but not so clean.
You fly, invoke the Gods; then turning, stop
To rail; she singing, still whirls on her Mop.
Not yet, the Dust had shun'd th' unequal Strife,
But aided by the Wind, fought still for Life;
And wafted with its Foe by violent Gust,
'Twas doubtful which was Rain, and which was Dust.
Ah! where must needy Poet seek for Aid,
When Dust and Rain at once his Coat invade;
Sole Coat, where Dust cemented by the Rain,
Erects the Nap, and leaves a cloudy Stain.

Now in contiguous Drops the Flood comes down,
Threat'ning with Deluge this *Devoted* Town.
To Shops in Crouds the dagled Females fly,
Pretend to cheapen Goods, but nothing buy.
The Templer spruce, while ev'ry Spout's a-broach,
Stays till 'tis fair, yet seems to call a Coach.
The tuck'd-up Sempstress walks with hasty Strides,
While Streams run down her oil'd Umbrella's Sides.
Here various Kinds by various Fortunes led,
Commence Acquaintance underneath a Shed.
Triumphant Tories, and desponding Whigs,
Forget their Fewds, and join to save their Wigs.
Box'd in a Chair the Beau impatient sits,
While Spouts run clatt'ring o'er the Roof by Fits;
And ever and anon with frightful Din
The Leather sounds, he trembles from within.
So when *Troy* Chair-men bore the Wooden Steed,
Pregnant with *Greeks*, impatient to be freed,
(Those Bully *Greeks*, who, as the Moderns do,
Instead of paying Chair-men, run them thro'.)
Laoco'n struck the Outside with his Spear,
And each imprison'd Hero quak'd for Fear.

Now from all Parts the swelling Kennels flow,
And bear their Trophies with them as they go:
Filth of all Hues and Odours seem to tell
What Streets they sail'd from, by the Sight and Smell.
They, as each Torrent drives, with rapid Force
From *Smithfield*, or St. *Pulchre's* shape their Course,
And in huge Confluent join at *Snow-Hill* Ridge,
Fall from the *Conduit* prone to *Holborn-Bridge.*
Sweepings from Butchers Stalls, Dung, Guts, and Blood,
Drown'd Puppies, stinking Sprats, all drench'd in Mud,
Dead Cats and Turnip-Tops come tumbling down the Flood.

depends, is imminent; *sink*, sewer; *aches*, pronounced 'aitches'; *quean*, slut;
devoted, doomed; *cheapen*, haggle; *templer*, law student; *chair*, sedan chair;
kennels, gutters.

5

from Cadenus and Vanessa

[. . .] In a glad Hour *Lucina*'s Aid
Produc'd on Earth a wond'rous Maid,
On whom the Queen of Love was bent
To try a new Experiment:
She threw her Law-books on the Shelf,
And thus debated with herself.

   Since Men alledge they ne'er can find
Those Beauties in a Female Mind,
Which raise a Flame that will endure
For ever, uncorrupt and pure;
If 'tis with Reason they complain,
This Infant shall restore my Reign.
I'll search where ev'ry Virtue dwells,
From Courts inclusive, down to Cells,
What Preachers talk, or Sages write,
These I will gather and unite,
And represent them to Mankind
Collected in that Infant's Mind.

   This said, she plucks in Heav'ns high Bow'rs
A Sprig of *Amaranthine* Flow'rs,
In Nectar thrice infuses Bays,
Three times refin'd in *Titan*'s Rays:
Then calls the *Graces* to her Aid,
And sprinkles thrice the new-born Maid.
From whence the tender Skin assumes
A Sweetness above all Perfumes;
From whence a Cleanliness remains,
Incapable of outward Stains;
From whence that Decency of Mind,
So lovely in the Female Kind,
Where not one careless Thought intrudes,
Less modest than the Speech of Prudes;

Where never Blush was call'd in Aid,
That spurious Virtue in a Maid,
A Virtue but at second-hand;
They blush because they understand.

The *Graces* next wou'd act their Part,
And shew'd but little of their Art;
Their Work was half already done,
The Child with native Beauty shone,
The outward Form no Help requir'd:
Each breathing on her thrice, inspir'd
That gentle, soft, engaging Air,
Which in old Times adorn'd the Fair;
And said, '*Vanessa* be the Name,
By which thou shalt be known to Fame:
'*Vanessa*, by the Gods enroll'd:
'Her Name on Earth — shall not be told.' [. . .]

The Goddess thus pronounc'd her Doom:
When, lo! *Vanessa* in her Bloom,
Advanc'd like *Atalanta's* Star,
But rarely seen, and seen from far:
In a new World with Caution stept,
Watch'd all the Company she kept,
Well knowing from the Books she read
What dangerous Paths young Virgins tread;
Wou'd seldom at the Park appear,
Nor saw the Play-House twice a Year;
Yet not incurious, was inclin'd
To know the Converse of Mankind.

First issu'd from Perfumers Shops
A Croud of fashionable Fops;
They ask'd her, how she lik'd the Play,
Then told the Tattle of the Day,
A Duel fought last Night at Two,
About a Lady — You know who;

Mention'd a new *Italian*, come
Either from *Muscovy* or *Rome*;
Gave Hints of who and who's together;
Then fell to talking of the Weather:
Last Night was so extremely fine,
The Ladies walk'd till after Nine.
Then in soft Voice and Speech absurd,
With Nonsense ev'ry second Word,
With Fustian from exploded Plays,
They celebrate her Beauty's Praise,
Run o'er their Cant of stupid Lies,
And tell the Murders of her Eyes.

   With silent Scorn *Vanessa* sat,
Scarce list'ning to their idle Chat;
Further than sometimes by a Frown,
When they grew pert, to pull them down.
At last she spitefully was bent
To try their Wisdom's full Extent;
And said, she valu'd nothing less
Than Titles, Figure, Shape, and Dress;
That, Merit should be chiefly plac'd
In Judgment, Knowledge, Wit, and Taste;
And these, she offer'd to dispute,
Alone distinguish'd Man from Brute:
That, present Times have no Pretence
To Virtue, in the Noblest Sense,
By *Greeks* and *Romans* understood,
To perish for our Country's Good.
She nam'd the antient Heroes round,
Explain'd for what they were renown'd;
Then spoke with Censure, or Applause,
Of foreign Customs, Rites, and Laws;
Thro' Nature, and thro' Art she rang'd,
And gracefully her Subject chang'd:
In vain: her Hearers had no share

In all she spoke, except to stare.
Their Judgment was upon the Whole,
– That Lady is the dullest Soul –
Then tipt their Forehead in a Jeer,
As who should say – she wants it here;
She may be handsome, young and rich,
But none will burn her for a Witch.

    A Party next of glitt'ring Dames,
From round the Purlieus of *St. James*,
Came early, out of pure Good-will,
To see the Girl in Deshabille.
Their Clamour 'lighting from their Chairs,
Grew louder, all the Way up Stairs;
At Entrance loudest, where they found
The Room with Volumes litter'd round
Vanessa held *Montaigne*, and read,
Whilst Mrs. *Susan* comb'd her Head:
They call'd for Tea and Chocolate,
And fell into their usual Chat,
Discoursing with important Face,
On Ribbons, Fans, and Gloves and Lace;
Shew'd Patterns just from *India* brought,
And gravely ask'd her what she thought,
Whether the Red or Green were best,
And what they cost? *Vanessa* guess'd,
As came into her Fancy first,
Nam'd half the Rates, and lik'd the worst,
To Scandal next — What aukward Thing
Was that, last *Sunday* in the Ring?
— I'm sorry *Mopsa* breaks so fast;
I said her Face would never last.
Corinna with that youthful Air,
Is thirty, and a Bit to spare.
Her Fondness for a certain Earl
Began, when I was but a Girl.

Phyllis, who but a Month ago
Was marry'd to the *Tunbridge* Beau,
I saw coquetting t'other Night
In publick with that odious Knight.

    They railly'd next *Vanessa*'s Dress;
That Gown was made for Old Queen *Bess*.
Dear Madam, Let me set your Head:
Don't you intend to put on Red?
A Pettycoat without a Hoop!
Sure, you are not asham'd to stoop;
With handsome Garters at your Knees,
No matter what a Fellow sees.

    Fill'd with Disdain, with Rage inflam'd,
Both of her self and Sex asham'd,
The Nymph stood silent out of spight,
Nor wou'd vouchsafe to set them right.
Away the fair Detractors went,
And gave, by turns, their Censures Vent.
She's not so handsome, in my Eyes:
For Wit, I wonder where it lies.
She's fair and clean, and that's the most;
But why proclaim her for a Toast?
A Baby Face, no Life, no Airs,
But what she learnt at Country Fairs;
Scarce knows what Diff'rence is between
Rich *Flanders* Lace, and Colberteen.
I'll undertake my little *Nancy*
In Flounces has a better Fancy.
With all her Wit, I wou'd not ask
Her Judgment, how to buy a Mask.
We begg'd her but to patch her Face,
She never hit one proper Place;
Which every Girl at Five Years old
Can do as soon as she is told.
I own, that out-of-fashion Stuff

Becomes the *Creature* well enough.
The Girl might pass, if we cou'd get her
To know the World a little better.
(*To know the World!* a modern Phrase,
For Visits, Ombre, Balls and Plays.) [. . .]

    Yet some of either Sex, endow'd
With Gifts superior to the Crowd,
With Virtue, Knowledge, Taste and Wit,
She condescended to admit:
With pleasing Arts she could reduce
Mens Talents to their proper Use;
And with Address each Genius held
To that wherein it most excell'd;
Thus making others Wisdom known,
Cou'd please them, and improve her own.
A modest Youth said something new,
She plac'd it in the strongest View.
All humble Worth she strove to raise;
Would not be prais'd, yet lov'd to praise.
The Learned met with free Approach,
Although they came not in a Coach.
Some Clergy too she wou'd allow,
Nor quarrell'd at their aukward Bow.
But this was for *Cadenus*' sake;
A Gownman of a diff'rent Make;
Whom *Pallas*, once *Vanessa*'s Tutor,
Had fix'd on for her Coadjutor. [. . .]

    Cupid, tho' all his Darts were lost,
Yet still resolv'd to spare no Cost;
He could not answer to his Fame
The Triumphs of that stubborn Dame,
A Nymph so hard to be subdu'd,
Who neither was Coquette nor Prude.
I find, says he, she wants a Doctor,
Both to adore her and instruct her;

I'll give her what she most admires,
Among those venerable Sires.
Cadenus is a Subject fit,
Grown old in Politicks and Wit;
Caress'd by Ministers of State,
Of half Mankind the Dread and Hate.
Whate'er Vexations Love attend,
She need no Rivals apprehend.
Her Sex, with universal Voice,
Must laugh at her capricious Choice.

   Cadenus many things had writ;
Vanessa much esteem'd his Wit,
And call'd for his Poetick Works;
Mean time the Boy in secret lurks,
And while the Book was in her Hand,
The Urchin from his private Stand
Took Aim, and shot with all his Strength
A Dart of such prodigious Length,
It pierc'd the feeble Volume thro',
And deep transfix'd her Bosom too.
Some Lines, more moving than the rest,
Stuck to the Point that pierc'd her Breast;
And, born directly to the Heart,
With Pains unknown increas'd her Smart.

   Vanessa, not in Years a Score,
Dreams of a Gown of forty-four;
Imaginary Charms can find,
In Eyes with Reading.almost blind;
Cadenus now no more appears
Declin'd in Health, advanc'd in Years.
She fancies Musick in his Tongue,
Nor further looks, but thinks him young.
What Mariner is not afraid,
To venture in a Ship decay'd?
What Planter will attempt to yoke

A Sapling with a falling Oak?
As Years increase, she brighter shines,
Cadenus with each Day declines,
And he must fall a Prey to Time,
While she continues in her Prime.

    Cadenus, common Forms apart,
In every Scene had kept his Heart;
Had sigh'd and languish'd, vow'd, and writ,
For Pastime, or to shew his Wit;
But Time, and Books, and State Affairs
Had spoil'd his fashionable Airs;
He now cou'd praise, esteem, approve,
But understood not what was Love.
His Conduct might have made him styl'd
A Father, and the Nymph his Child.
That innocent Delight he took
To see the Virgin mind her Book,
Was but the Master's secret Joy
In School to hear the finest Boy.
Her Knowledge with her Fancy grew;
She hourly press'd for something new;
Ideas came into her Mind
So fast, his Lessons lagg'd behind:
She reason'd, without plodding long,
Nor ever gave her Judgment wrong.
But now a sudden Change was wrought,
She minds no longer what he taught.
Cadenus was amaz'd to find
Such Marks of a distracted Mind;
For tho' she seem'd to listen more
To all he spoke, than e'er before;
He found her Thoughts would absent range,
Yet guess'd not whence could spring the Change.
And first he modestly conjectures
His Pupil might be tir'd with Lectures;

13

Which help'd to mortify his Pride,
Yet gave him not the Heart to chide;
But in a mild dejected Strain,
At last he ventur'd to complain:
Said, she shou'd be no longer teiz'd;
Might have her Freedom when she pleas'd:
Was now convinc'd he acted wrong,
To hide her from the World so long;
And in dull Studies to engage
One of her tender Sex and Age.
That ev'ry Nymph with Envy own'd,
How she might shine in the *Grand-Monde*,
And ev'ry Shepherd was undone
To see her cloister'd like a Nun.
This was a visionary Scheme,
He wak'd, and found it but a Dream;
A Project far above his Skill,
For Nature must be Nature still.
If he was bolder than became
A Scholar to a Courtly Dame,
She might excuse a Man of Letters;
Thus Tutors often treat their Betters.
And since his Talk offensive grew,
He came to take his last Adieu.

Vanessa, fill'd with just Disdain,
Wou'd still her Dignity maintain,
Instructed from her early Years
To scorn the Art of Female Tears.

Had he employ'd his Time so long,
To teach her what was Right or Wrong,
Yet cou'd such Notions entertain,
That all his Lectures were in vain?
She own'd the wand'ring of her Thoughts,
But he must answer for her Faults.
She well remember'd to her Cost,

That all his Lessons were not lost.
Two Maxims she could still produce,
And sad Experience taught their Use:
That Virtue, pleas'd by being shown,
Knows nothing which it dare not own;
Can make us without Fear disclose
Our inmost Secrets to our Foes:
That common Forms were not design'd
Directors to a noble Mind.
Now, said the Nymph, I'll let you see
My Actions with your Rules agree,
That I can vulgar Forms despise,
And have no Secrets to disguise.
I knew by what you said and writ,
How dang'rous Things were Men of Wit,
You caution'd me against their Charms,
But never gave me equal Arms:
Your Lessons found the weakest Part,
Aim'd at the Head, but reach'd the Heart.

Cadenus felt within him rise
Shame, Disappointment, Guilt, Surprize.
He knew not how to reconcile
Such Language, with her usual Style:
And yet her Words were so exprest,
He cou'd not hope she spoke in Jest.
His Thoughts had wholly been confin'd
To form and cultivate her Mind.
He hardly knew, 'till he was told,
Whether the Nymph were Young or Old;
Had met her in a publick Place,
Without distinguishing her Face.
Much less could his declining Age
Vanessa's earliest Thoughts engage.
And if her Youth Indifference met,
His Person must Contempt beget.

Or grant her Passion be sincere,
How shall his Innocence be clear?
Appearances were all so strong,
The World must think him in the Wrong;
Wou'd say, He made a treach'rous Use
Of Wit, to flatter and seduce:
The Town wou'd swear he had betray'd,
By Magick Spells, the harmless Maid;
And ev'ry Beau wou'd have his Jokes,
That Scholars were like other Folks:
That when Platonick Flights were over,
The Tutor turn'd a mortal Lover.
So tender of the Young and Fair?
It shew'd a true Paternal Care –
Five thousand Guineas in her Purse?
The Doctor might have fancy'd worse. – [. . .]

     But not to dwell on Things minute,
Vanessa finish'd the Dispute,
Brought weighty Arguments to prove
That Reason was her Guide in Love.
She thought he had himself describ'd,
His Doctrines when she first imbib'd;
What he had planted, now was grown;
His Virtues she might call her own;
As he approves, as he dislikes,
Love or Contempt, her Fancy strikes.
Self-Love, in Nature rooted fast,
Attends us first, and leaves us last:
Why she likes him, admire not at her,
She loves herself, and that's the Matter.
How was her Tutor wont to praise
The Genius's of ancient Days!
(Those Authors he so oft had nam'd
For Learning, Wit, and Wisdom fam'd;)
Was struck with Love, Esteem, and Awe,

For Persons whom he never saw.
Suppose *Cadenus* flourish'd then,
He must adore such God-like Men.
If one short Volume cou'd comprise
All that was witty, learn'd, and wise,
How wou'd it be esteem'd, and read,
Altho' the Writer long were dead?
If such an Author were alive,
How all wou'd for his Friendship strive;
And come in Crowds to see his Face:
And this she takes to be her Case.
Cadenus answers every End,
The Book, the Author, and the Friend.
The utmost her Desires will reach,
Is but to learn what he can teach;
His Converse is a System, fit
Alone to fill up all her Wit;
While ev'ry Passion of her Mind
In him is center'd and confin'd.

   Love can with Speech inspire a Mute,
And taught Vanessa to dispute.
This Topick, never touch'd before,
Display'd her Eloquence the more:
Her Knowledge, with such Pains acquir'd,
By this new Passion grew inspir'd.
Thro' this she made all Objects pass,
Which gave a Tincture o'er the Mass:
As Rivers, tho' they bend and twine,
Still to the Sea their Course incline;
Or, as Philosophers, who find
Some fav'rite System to their Mind,
In ev'ry Point to make it fit,
Will force all Nature to submit.

   Cadenus, who cou'd ne'er suspect
His Lessons wou'd have such Effect,

Or be so artfully apply'd,
Insensibly came on her Side;
It was an unforeseen Event,
Things took a Turn he never meant.
Whoe'er excels in what we prize,
Appears a Hero to our Eyes;
Each Girl when pleas'd with what is taught,
Will have the Teacher in her Thought.
When Miss delights in her Spinnet,
A Fidler may a Fortune get;
A Blockhead with melodious Voice
In Boarding-Schools can have his Choice;
And oft' the Dancing-Master's Art
Climbs from the Toe to touch the Heart.
In Learning let a Nymph delight,
The Pedant gets a Mistress by't.
Cadenus, to his Grief and Shame,
Cou'd scarce oppose *Vanessa*'s Flame;
But tho' her Arguments were strong,
At least, cou'd hardly wish them wrong.
Howe'er it came, he cou'd not tell,
But, sure, she never talk'd so well.
His Pride began to interpose,
Preferr'd before a Crowd of Beaux,
So bright a Nymph to come unsought,
Such Wonder by his Merit wrought;
'Tis Merit must with her prevail,
He never knew her Judgment fail,
She noted all she ever read,
And had a most discerning Head.

  'Tis an old Maxim in the Schools,
That Vanity's the Food of Fools;
Yet now and then your Men of Wit
Will condescend to take a Bit.

So when *Cadenus* could not hide,
He chose to justify his Pride;
Constr'ing the Passion she had shown,
Much to her Praise, more to his Own.
Nature in him had Merit plac'd,
In her, a most judicious Taste.
Love, hitherto a transient Guest,
Ne'er held Possession of his Breast;
So, long attending at the Gate,
Disdain'd to enter in so late.
Love, why do we one Passion call?
When 'tis a Compound of them all;
Where hot and cold, where sharp and sweet,
In all their Equipages meet;
Where Pleasures mix'd with Pains appear,
Sorrow with Joy, and Hope with Fear;
Wherein his Dignity and Age
Forbid *Cadenus* to engage.
But Friendship in its greatest Height,
A constant, rational Delight,
On Virtue's Basis fix'd to last,
When Love's Allurements long are past;
Which gently warms, but cannot burn;
He gladly offers in return:
His Want of Passion will redeem,
With Gratitude, Respect, Esteem:
With that Devotion we bestow,
When Goddesses appear below.

While thus *Cadenus* entertains
Vanessa in exalted Strains,
The Nymph in sober Words intreats
A Truce with all sublime Conceits.
For why such Raptures, Flights, and Fancies,
To her, who durst not read Romances;
In lofty Style to make Replies,

Which he had taught her to despise.
But when her Tutor will affect
Devotion, Duty, and Respect,
He fairly abdicates his Throne,
The Government is now her own;
He has a Forfeiture incurr'd,
She vows to take him at his Word,
And hopes he will not think it strange
If both shou'd now their Stations change.
The Nymph will have her Turn, to be
The Tutor; and the Pupil, he:
Tho' she already can discern,
Her Scholar is not apt to learn;
Or wants Capacity to reach
The Science she designs to teach:
Wherein his Genius was below
The Skill of ev'ry common Beau;
Who, tho' he cannot spell, is wise
Enough to read a Lady's Eyes;
And will each accidental Glance
Interpret for a kind Advance.

But what Success *Vanessa* met,
Is to the World a Secret yet:
Whether the Nymph, to please her Swain,
Talks in a high Romantick Strain;
Or whether he at last descends
To like with less Seraphick Ends;
Or, to compound the Business, whether
They temper Love and Books together;
Must never to Mankind be told,
Nor shall the conscious Muse unfold.

Italian, opera singer; *Mrs Susan*, generic maid; *Ring*, Hyde Park; *breaks*, fails;
Tunbridge, the spa; *rallied*, teased; *red*, rouge; *Colbertine*, French lace; *mask*,
veil; *patch*, with beauty spots; *ombre*, card game.

Horace, *Lib.* 2. *Sat.* 6

Part of it imitated

I often wish'd, that I had clear
For Life, six hundred Pounds a Year,
A handsome House to lodge a Friend,
A River at my Garden's End,
A Terras Walk, and half a Rood
Of Land set out to plant a Wood.

   Well, now I have all this and more,
I ask not to increase my Store,
And should be perfectly content,
Could I but live on this side *Trent*;
Nor cross the *Channel* twice a Year,
To spend six Months with *Statesmen* here.

   I must by all means come to Town,
'Tis for the Service of the Crown.
'*Lewis*; the *Dean* will be of Use,
'Send for him up, take no Excuse.'
The Toil, the Danger of the Seas;
Great Ministers ne'er think of these;
Or let it cost Five hundred Pound,
No matter where the Money's found;
It is but so much more in Debt,
And that they ne'er consider'd yet.

   'Good Mr. *Dean* go change your Gown,
'Let my Lord know you're come to Town.'
I hurry me in haste away,
Not thinking it is Levee-Day;
And find his Honour in a Pound,
Hemm'd by a triple Circle round,
Chequer'd with Ribbons blew and green;
How should I thrust my self between?

Some Wag observes me thus perplext,
And smiling, whispers to the next,
'I thought the *Dean* had been too proud,
'To justle here among a Crowd.'
Another in a surly Fit,
Tells me I have more Zeal than Wit,
'So eager to express your Love,
'You ne'er consider whom you shove,
'But rudely press before a Duke.'
I own, I'm pleas'd with this Rebuke,
And take it kindly meant to show
What I desire the World should know.

   I get a Whisper, and withdraw,
When twenty Fools I never saw
Come with Petitions fairly pen'd,
Desiring I would stand their Friend.

   This, humbly offers me his Case:
That, begs my Interest for a Place.
A hundred other Men's Affairs
Like Bees, are humming in my Ears.
'To morrow my Appeal comes on,
'Without your Help the Cause is gone —'
The Duke expects my Lord and you,
About some great Affair, at Two —
'Put my Lord *Bolingbroke* in Mind,
'To get my Warrant quickly signed:
'Consider, 'tis my first Request. —'
Be satisfy'd, I'll do my best: —
Then presently he falls to teize,
'You may for certain, if you please;
'I doubt not, if his Lordship knew —
'And Mr. *Dean*, one Word from you —'

   'Tis (let me see) three Years and more,
(*October* next, it will be four)

Since HARLEY bid me first attend,
And chose me for an humble Friend;
Would take me in his Coach to chat,
And question me of this and that;
As, 'What's a-Clock?' And, 'How's the Wind?'
'Whose Chariot's that we left behind?'
Or gravely try to read the Lines
Writ underneath the Country *Signs*;
Or, 'Have you nothing new to day
'From *Pope*, from *Parnel*, or from *Gay*?'
Such Tattle often entertains
My Lord and me as far as *Stains*,
As once a week we travel down
To *Windsor*, and again to Town,
Where all that passes, *inter nos*,
Might be proclaim'd at *Charing-Cross*.

Yet some I know with Envy swell,
Because they see me us'd so well:
'How think you of our Friend the *Dean*?
'I wonder what some People mean;
'My Lord and he are grown so great,
'Always together, *tête à tête*:
'What, they admire him for his Jokes —
'See but the Fortune of some Folks!'
There flies about a strange Report
Of some Express arriv'd at Court;
I'm stopt by all the Fools I meet,
And catechis'd in ev'ry Street.
'You, Mr. *Dean* frequent the Great;
'Inform us, will the Emp'ror treat?
'Or do the Prints and Papers lye?'
Faith Sir, you know as much as I.
'Ah Doctor, how you love to jest?
' 'Tis now no Secret' – I protest
'Tis one to me. – 'Then, tell us, pray

'When are the Troops to have their Pay?'
And, though I solemnly declare
I know no more than my *Lord Mayor*,
They stand amaz'd, and think me grown
The closest Mortal ever known.

Thus in a Sea of Folly tost,
My choicest Hours of Life are lost:
Yet always wishing to retreat;
Oh, could I see my Country Seat.
There leaning near a gentle Brook,
Sleep, or peruse some antient Book;
And there in sweet Oblivion drown
Those Cares that haunt a Court and Town.

Trent, i.e. near London; *Channel*, St George's Channel, Irish Sea.

In Sickness

Written soon after the Author's coming to live in Ireland,
upon the Queen's Death, October 1714

'Tis true, – then why should I repine,
To see my Life so fast decline?
But, why obscurely here alone?
Where I am neither lov'd nor known.
My State of Health none care to learn;
My Life is here no Soul's Concern.
And, those with whom I now converse,
Without a Tear will tend my Herse.
Remov'd from kind *Arbuthnot*'s Aid,
Who knows his Art but not the Trade;
Preferring his Regard for me
Before his Credit or his Fee.
Some formal Visits, Looks, and Words,
What meer Humanity affords,
I meet perhaps from three or four,
From whom I once expected more;
Which those who tend the Sick for pay
Can act as decently as they.
But, no obliging, tender Friend
To help at my approaching End,
My Life is now a Burthen grown
To others, e'er it be my own.

   Ye formal Weepers for the Sick,
In your last Offices be quick:
And spare my absent Friends the Grief
To hear, yet give me no Relief;
Expir'd To-day, entomb'd To-morrow,
When known, will save a double Sorrow.

Mary the Cook-Maid's Letter to Dr Sheridan

Well; if ever I saw such another Man since my Mother bound
    my Head,
You a Gentleman! marry come up, I wonder where you were
    bred?
I am sure such Words does not become a Man of your Cloth,
I would not give such Language to a Dog, faith and troth.
Yes; you call'd my Master a Knave: Fie Mr *Sheridan*, 'tis a
    Shame
For a Parson, who shou'd know better Things, to come out
    with such a Name.
Knave in your Teeth, Mr *Sheridan*, 'tis both a Shame and a
    Sin,
And the Dean my Master is an honester Man than you and
    all your kin:
He has more Goodness in his little Finger, than you have in
    your whole Body,
My Master is a parsonable Man, and not a spindle-shank'd
    hoddy doddy.
And now whereby I find you would fain make an Excuse,
Because my Master one Day in anger call'd you Goose.
Which, and I am sure I have been his Servant four Years
    since *October*,
And he never call'd me worse than Sweet-heart drunk or
    sober:
Not that I know his Reverence was ever concern'd to my
    knowledge,
Tho' you and your Come-rogues keep him out so late in your
    wicked Colledge.

You say you will eat Grass on his Grave: a Christian eat
    Grass!
Whereby you now confess your self to be a Goose or an Ass:
But that's as much as to say, that my Master should die
    before ye,

Well, well, that's as God pleases, and I don't believe that's a
  true Story,
And so say I told you so, and you may go tell my Master;
  what care I?
And I don't care who knows it, 'tis all one to *Mary*.
Every body knows, that I love to tell Truth and shame the
  Devil,
I am but a poor Servant, but I think Gentle folks should be
  civil.
Besides, you found fault with our Vittles one Day that you
  was here,
I remember it was upon a *Tuesday*, of all Days in the Year.
And *Saunders* the Man says, you are always jesting and
  mocking,
Mary said he, (one Day, as I was mending my Master's
  Stocking,)
My Master is so fond of that Minister that keeps the School;
I thought my Master a wise Man, but that Man makes him a
  Fool.
Saunders said I, I would rather than a Quart of Ale,
He would come into our Kitchin, and I would pin a
  Dishclout to his Tail.
And now I must go, and get *Saunders* to direct this Letter,
For I write but a sad Scrawl, but my Sister *Marget* she writes
  better.
Well, but I must run and make the Bed before my Master
  comes from Pray'rs,
And see now, it strikes ten, and I hear him coming up Stairs:
Whereof I cou'd say more to your Verses, if I could write
  written hand,
And so I remain in a civil way, your Servant to command,
                                                    Mary.

concerned, drunk; *Saunders*, Swift's servant, Alexander McGee; *written*,
cursive, joined-up.

The Author's manner of Living

On rainy Days alone I dine,
Upon a Chick, and Pint of Wine,
On rainy Days, I dine alone,
And pick my Chicken to the Bone:
But this my Servants much enrages,
No Scraps remain to save Board-wages.
In Weather fine I nothing spend,
But often spunge upon a Friend:
Yet where He's not so rich as I;
I pay my Club, and so GOD b'y' —.

Club, share.

On Stella's Birth-day
Written AD 1718–[19]

Stella this Day is thirty four,
(We shan't dispute a Year or more)
However Stella, be not troubled,
Although thy Size and Years are doubled,
Since first I saw Thee at Sixteen
The brightest Virgin on the Green,
So little is thy Form declin'd
Made up so largly in thy Mind.
Oh, would it please the Gods to split
Thy Beauty, Size, and Years, and Wit,
No Age could furnish out a Pair
Of Nymphs so gracefull, Wise and fair
With half the Lustre of Your Eyes,
With half your Wit, your Years and Size:
And then before it grew too late,
How should I beg of gentle Fate,
(That either Nymph might have her Swain,)
To split my Worship too in twain.

from To Stella,
Who Collected and Transcribed his Poems

As when a lofty Pile is rais'd,
We never hear the Workmen prais'd,
Who bring the Lime, or place the Stones;
But all admire *Inigo Jones*:
So if this Pile of scatter'd Rhymes
Should be approv'd in After-times,
If it both pleases and endures,
The Merit and the Praise are yours.

The Run upon the Bankers

Written AD 1720

The bold Encroachers on the Deep,
Gain by Degrees huge Tracts of Land,
'Till Neptune with a Gen'ral Sweep
Turns all again to barren Strand.

    The Multitude's Capricious Pranks
Are said to represent the Seas,
Breaking the Bankers and the Banks,
Resume their own when e'er they please.

    Money, the Life-blood of the Nation,
Corrupts and stagnates in the Veins,
Unless a proper Circulation
Its Motion and its Heat maintains.

    Because 'tis Lordly not to pay,
Quakers and Aldermen, in State,
Like Peers, have Levees ev'ry Day
Of Duns, attending at their Gate.

    We want our Money on the Nail;
The Banker's ruin'd if he pays;
They seem to act an Ancient Tale,
The Birds are met to strip the Jays.

    Riches, the Wisest Monarch sings,
Make Pinions for themselves to fly,
They fly like Bats, on Parchment Wings,
And Geese their silver Plumes supply.

    No Money left for squandring Heirs!
Bills turn the Lenders into Debters,
The Wish of Nero now is Theirs,
That, they had never known their Letters.

Conceive the Works of Midnight Hags,
Tormenting Fools behind their Backs;
Thus Bankers o'er their Bills and Bags
Sit squeezing Images of Wax.

Conceive the whole Enchantment broke,
The Witches left in open Air,
With Pow'r no more than other Folk,
Expos'd with all their Magick Ware.

So Pow'rful are a Banker's Bills
Where Creditors demand their Due;
They break up Counter, Doors, and Tills,
And leave his empty Chests in View.

Thus when an Earthquake lets in Light
Upon the god of Gold and Hell,
Unable to endure the Sight,
He hides within his darkest Cell.

As when a Conj'rer takes a Lease
From Satan for a Term of Years,
The Tenant's in a Dismal Case
When e'er the bloody Bond appears.

A baited Banker thus desponds,
From his own Hand foresees his Fall,
They have his Soul who have his Bonds,
'Tis like the Writing on the Wall.

How will the Caitiff Wretch be scar'd
When first he finds himself awake
At the last Trumpet, unprepar'd,
And all his Grand Account to make?

For in that Universal Call
Few Bankers will to Heav'n be Mounters:
They'll cry, Ye Shops, upon us fall
Conceal, and cover us, Ye Counters.

When Other Hands the Scales shall hold,
And They in Men and Angels Sight
Produc'd with all their Bills and Gold,
Weigh'd in the Ballance, and found Light.

The Description of an Irish Feast, translated almost literally out of the Original Irish

Translated in the Year 1720

O'Rourk's noble Fare
  Will ne'er be forgot,
By those who were there,
  Or those who were not.
His Revels to keep,
  We sup and we dine,
On seven Score Sheep,
  Fat Bullocks and Swine.
Usquebaugh to our Feast
  In Pails was brought up,
An Hundred at least,
  And a Madder our Cup.
O there is the Sport,
  We rise with the Light,
In disorderly Sort,
  From snoring all Night.
O how was I trick't,
  My Pipe it was broke,
My Pocket was pick't,
  I lost my new Cloak.
I'm rifled, quoth *Nell*,
  Of Mantle and Kercher,
Why then fare them well,
  The De'el take the Searcher.
Come, Harper, strike up,
  But first by your Favour,
Boy, give us a Cup;
  Ay, this has some Savour:
O *Rourk*'s jolly Boys
  Ne'er dream't of the Matter,
Till rowz'd by the Noise,

And musical Clatter,
They bounce from their Nest,
   No longer will tarry,
They rise ready drest,
   Without one *Ave Mary*.
They dance in a Round,
   Cutting Capers and Ramping,
A Mercy the Ground
   Did not burst with their stamping.
The Floor is all wet
   With Leaps and with Jumps,
While the Water and Sweat,
   Splish, splash in their Pumps.
Bless you late and early,
   Laughlin O Enagin,
By my Hand, you dance rarely,
   Margery Grinagin.
Bring Straw for our Bed,
   Shake it down to the Feet,
Then over us spread,
   The winnowing Sheet.
To show, I don't flinch,
   Fill the Bowl up again,
Then give us a Pinch
   Of your Sneezing; *a Yean*.
Good Lord, what a Sight,
   After all their good Cheer,
For People to fight
   In the Midst of their Beer:
They rise from their Feast,
   And hot are their brains,
A Cubit at least
   The Length of their Skeans.
What Stabs and what Cuts,
   What clatt'ring of Sticks,
What Strokes on the Guts,

What Bastings and Kicks!
With Cudgels of Oak,
    Well harden'd in Flame,
An hundred Heads broke,
    An hundred struck lame.
You Churle, I'll maintain
    My Father built *Lusk*,
The Castle of *Slain*,
    And *Carrickdrumrusk*:
The Earl of *Kildare*,
    And *Moynalta*, his Brother,
As great as they are,
    I was nurs'd by their Mother.
Ask that of old *Madam*,
    She'll tell you who's who,
As far up as *Adam*,
    She knows it is true,
Come down with that Beam,
    If Cudgels are scarce,
A Blow on the Weam,
    Or a Kick on the Arse.

Usquebaugh, whiskey; *madder*, wooden bowl; *ramping*, romping; *a Yean*,
woman, (the 'a' is vocative); *skenes*, daggers; *weam*, stomach.

Stella's Birth-Day
Written AD 1720–21

All Travellers at first incline
Where'e'er they see the fairest Sign,
And if they find the Chambers neat,
And like the Liquor and the Meat
Will call again and recommend
The Angel-Inn to ev'ry Friend:
What though the Painting grows decayd
The House will never loose it's Trade;
Nay, though the treach'rous Tapster Thomas
Hangs a new Angel two doors from us
As fine as Dawbers Hands can make it
In hopes that Strangers may mistake it,
We think it both a Shame and Sin
To quit the true old Angel-Inn.

Now, this is Stella's Case in Fact;
An Angel's Face, a little crack't;
(Could Poets or could Painters fix
How Angels look at thirty six)
This drew us in at first to find
In such a Form an Angel's Mind
And ev'ry Virtue now supplyes
The fainting Rays of Stella's Eyes:
See, at her Levee crowding Swains
Whom Stella freely entertains
With Breeding, Humor, Wit, and Sense,
And puts them to so small Expence,
Their Minds so plentifully fills,
And makes such reasonable Bills
So little gets for what she gives
We really wonder how she lives;
And, had her Stock been less, no doubt
She must have long ago run out.

Then, who can think we'll quit the Place
When Doll hangs out a newer Face
Or stop and light at Cloe's Head
With Scraps and Leavings to be fed.
    Then Cloe, still go on to prate
Of thirty six, and thirty eight;
Pursue thy Trade of Scandall picking,
Your Hints that Stella is no Chickin,
Your Innuendo's when you tell us
That Stella loves to talk with Fellows
But let me warn you to believe
A Truth for which your Soul should grieve,
That, should you live to see the Day
When Stella's Locks must all be grey
When Age must print a furrow'd Trace
On ev'ry Feature of her Face;
Though you and all your senceless Tribe
Could Art or Time or Nature bribe
To make you look like Beauty's Queen
And hold for ever at fifteen:
No Bloom of Youth can ever blind
The Cracks and Wrinckles of your Mind,
All Men of Sense will pass your Dore
And crowd to Stella's at fourscore.

A Satirical Elegy
On the Death of a late Famous General

His Grace! impossible! what dead!
Of old age too, and in his bed!
And could that Mighty Warrior fall?
And so inglorious, after all!
Well, since he's gone, no matter how,
The last loud trump must wake him now:
And, trust me, as the noise grows stronger,
He'd wish to sleep a little longer.
And could he be indeed so old
As by the news-papers we're told?
Threescore, I think, is pretty high;
'Twas time in conscience he should die.
This world he cumber'd long enough;
He burnt his candle to the snuff;
And that's the reason, some folks think,
He left behind *so great a stink*.
Behold his funeral appears,
Nor widow's sighs, nor orphan's tears,
Wont at such times each heart to pierce,
Attend the progress of his herse.
But what of that, his friends may say,
He had those honours in his day.
True to his profit and his pride,
He made them weep before he dy'd.

   Come hither, all ye empty things,
Ye bubbles rais'd by breath of Kings;
Who float upon the tide of state,
Come hither, and behold your fate.
Let pride be taught by this rebuke,
How very mean a thing's a Duke;
From all his ill-got honours flung,
Turn'd to that dirt from whence he sprung.

Stella at Wood-Park,
A House of Charles Ford, *Esq; eight Miles from* Dublin

— Cuicunuqe; nocere volebat
Vestimenta dabat pretiosa.
Written in the Year 1723

Don *Carlos* in a merry Spight,
Did *Stella* to his House invite:
He entertain'd her half a Year
With gen'rous Wines and costly Chear.
Don *Carlos* made her chief Director,
That she might o'er the Servants hector.
In half a Week the Dame grew nice,
Got all things at the highest Price.
Now at the Table-Head she sits,
Presented with the nicest Bits:
She look'd on Partridges with scorn,
Except they tasted of the Corn:
A Haunch of Ven'son made her sweat,
Unless it had the right *Fumette*.
Don *Carlos* earnestly would beg,
Dear Madam, try this Pigeon's Leg;
Was happy when he could prevail
To make her only touch a Quail.
Through Candle-Light she view'd the Wine,
To see that ev'ry Glass was fine.
At last grown prouder than the Devil,
With feeding high, and Treatment civil,
Don *Carlos* now began to find
His Malice work as he design'd:
The Winter-Sky began to frown,
Poor *Stella* must pack off to Town.
From purling Streams and Fountains bubbling,
To *Liffy*'s stinking Tide in *Dublin*:
From wholesome Exercise and Air

To sossing in an easy Chair;
From Stomach sharp and hearty feeding,
To piddle like a Lady breeding:
From ruling there the Household singly,
To be directed here by *Dingly*:
From ev'ry Day a lordly Banquet,
To half a Joint, and God be thank it:
From ev'ry Meal *Pontack* in plenty,
To half a Pint one Day in twenty.
From *Ford* attending at her Call,
To visits of Archdeacon Wall[,]
From *Ford*, who thinks of nothing mean,
To the poor Doings of the Dean.
From growing Riche[r] with good Chear,
To running out by starving here.

    But now arrives the dismal Day:
She must return to *Ormond Key*:
The Coachman stopt, she lookt, and swore
The Rascal had mistook the Door:
At coming in you saw her stoop;
The Entry brusht against her Hoop:
Each Moment rising in her Airs,
She curst the narrow winding Stairs:
Began a Thousand Faults to spy;
The Ceiling hardly six Foot high;
The smutty Wainscot full of Cracks,
And half the Chairs with broken Backs:
Her Quarter's out at *Lady-Day*,
She vows she will no longer stay,
In Lodgings, like a poor *Grizette*,
While there are Lodgings to be lett.

    Howe'er, to keep her Spirits up,
She sent for Company to sup;
When all the while you might remark,
She strove in vain to ape *Wood-Park*.

Two Bottles call'd for, (half her Store;
The Cupboard could contain but four;)
A Supper worthy of her self,
Five *Nothings* in five Plates of *Delph*.

Thus, for a Week the Farce went on;
When all her Count[r]y-Savings gone,
She fell into her former Scene,
Small Beer, a Herring, and the Dean.

Thus, far in jest. Though now I fear
You think my jesting too severe:
But Poets when a Hint is new
Regard not whether false or true:
Yet Raillery gives no Offence,
Where Truth has not the least Pretence;
Nor can be more securely plac't
Than on a Nymph of *Stella*'s Taste.
I must confess, your Wine and Vittle
I was too hard upon *a little*;
Your Table neat, your Linnen fine;
And, though in Miniature, you shine,
Yet, when you sigh to leave *Wood-Park*,
The Scene, the Welcome, and the Spark,
To languish in this odious Town,
And pull your haughty Stomach down;
We think you quite mistake the Case;
The Virtue lies not in the Place:
For though my Raillery were true,
A Cottage is *Wood-Park* with you.

Quicunque . . ., 'If he wished to harm someone, he gave him costly clothes'
(Horace, *Epistles*); *Don Carlos*, Charles Ford; *fumette*, scent; *malice*, medicine;
sossing, lounging; *stomach*, appetite; *piddle*, pick at food; *breeding*, pregnant;
Pontac, a claret; *entry*, entrance hall; *quarter's out*, lease expires; *small*, weak;
spark, beau; *stomach*, disposition.

On Dreams
An Imitation of Petronius

Somnia quæ mentes ludunt volitantibus umbris, & c..

Those Dreams that on the silent Night intrude,
And with false flitting Shades our Minds delude,
Jove never sends us downward from the Skies,
Nor can they from infernal Mansions rise;
But all are meer Productions of the Brain,
And Fools consult Interpreters in vain.

For, when in Bed we rest our weary Limbs,
The Mind unburthen'd sports in various Whims,
The busy Head with mimick Art runs o'er
The Scenes and Actions of the Day before.

The drowsy Tyrant, by his Minions led,
To regal Rage devotes some Patriot's Head.
With equal Terrors, not with equal Guilt,
The Murd'rer dreams of all the Blood he spilt.

The Soldier smiling hears the Widows Cries,
And stabs the Son before the Mother's Eyes.
With like Remorse his Brother of the Trade,
The Butcher, feels the Lamb beneath his blade.

The Statesman rakes the Town to find a Plot,
And dreams of Forfeitures by Treason got.
Not less Tom-Turd-Man of true Statesman mold,
Collects the City Filth in search of Gold.

Orphans around his Bed the Lawyer sees,
And takes the Plaintiff's and Defendant's Fees.
His fellow Pick-Purse, watching for a Job,
Fancies his Fingers in the Cully's Fob.

The kind Physician grants the Husband's Prayers,
Or gives Relief to long-expecting Heirs.

The sleeping Hangman ties the fatal Noose,
Nor unsuccessful waits for dead Mens Shoes.

    The grave Divine with knotty Points perplext,
As if he were awake, nods o'er his Text:
While the sly Mountebank attends his Trade,
Harangues the Rabble, and is better paid.

    The hireling Senator of modern Days,
Bedaubs the guilty Great with nauseous Praise:
And *Dick* the Scavenger with equal Grace,
Flirts from his Cart the Mud in *Walpole*'s Face.

Somnia . . ., 'Dreams which fool the mind with flitting shadows'; *devotes*, condemns; *forfeitures*, confiscations; *cully*, fellow; *fob*, waistcoat pocket.

Stella's Birth-day, 1725

As when a beauteous Nymph decays
We say, she's past her Dancing Days;
So, Poets lose their Feet by Time,
And can no longer dance in Rhyme.
Your Annual Bard had rather chose
To celebrate your Birth in Prose;
Yet, merry Folks who want by chance
A Pair to make a Country Dance,
Call the Old Housekeeper, and get her
To fill a Place, for want of better;
While *Sheridan* is off the hooks,
And Friend *Delany* at his Books,
That *Stella* may avoid Disgrace
Once more the Dean supplies their Place.

Beauty and Wit, too sad a Truth,
Have always been confin'd to Youth;
The God of Wit, and Beauty's Queen,
He Twenty one, and She Fifteen:
No Poet ever sweetly sung,
Unless he were like *Phæbus*, young;
Nor ever Nymph inspir'd to Rhyme,
Unless, like *Venus*, in her Prime.
At Fifty six, if this be true,
Am I a Poet fit for you?
Or at the Age of Forty three,
Are you a Subject fit for me?
Adieu bright Wit, and radiant Eyes;
You must be grave, and I be wise.
Our Fate in vain we would oppose,
But I'll be still your Friend in Prose:
Esteem and Friendship to express,
Will not require Poetick Dress;

And if the Muse deny her Aid
To have them *sung*, they may be *said*.

But, *Stella* say, what evil Tongue
Reports you are no longer young?
That *Time* sits with his Scythe to mow
Where erst sate *Cupid* with his Bow;
That half your Locks are turn'd to Grey;
I'll ne'er believe a Word they say.
'Tis true, but let it not be known,
My Eyes are somewhat dimmish grown;
For Nature, always in the Right,
To your Decays adapts my Sight,
And Wrinkles undistinguish'd pass,
For I'm asham'd to use a Glass;
And till I see them with these Eyes,
Whoever says you have them, lyes.

No Length of Time can make you quit
Honour and Virtue, Sense and Wit,
Thus you may still be young to me,
While I can better *hear* than *see*;
Oh, ne'er may Fortune shew her Spight,
To make me *deaf*, and mend my *Sight*.

off the hooks, out of sorts.

To Quilca, a Country House in no very good Repair,
where the supposed Author, and some of his Friends,
spent a Summer, in the Year 1725

Let me my Properties explain,
A rotten Cabbin, dropping Rain;
Chimnies with Scorn rejecting Smoak;
Stools, Tables, Chairs, and Bed-stede broke:
Here Elements have lost their Uses,
Air ripens not, nor Earth produces:
In vain we make poor *Sheelah* toil,
Fire will not roast, nor Water boil.
Thro' all the Vallies, Hills, and Plains,
The Goddess *Want* in Triumph reigns;
And her chief Officers of State,
Sloth, *Dirt*, and *Theft* around her wait.

Stella's Birth-day
March 13, 1726/7

This Day, whate'er the Fates decree,
Shall still be kept with Joy by me:
This Day then, let us not be told,
That you are sick, and I grown old,
Nor think on our approaching Ills,
And talk of Spectacles and Pills;
To morrow will be Time enough
To hear such mortifying Stuff.
Yet, since from Reason may be brought
A better and more pleasing Thought,
Which can in spite of all Decays,
Support a few remaining Days:
From not the gravest of Divines,
Accept for once some serious Lines.

Although we now can form no more
Long Schemes of Life, as heretofore;
Yet you, while Time is running fast,
Can look with Joy on what is past.

Were future Happiness and Pain,
A mere Contrivance of the Brain,
As Atheists argue, to entice,
And fit their Proselytes for Vice;
(The only Comfort they propose,
To have Companions in their Woes.)
Grant this the Case, yet sure 'tis hard,
That Virtue, stil'd its own Reward,
And by all Sages understood
To be the chief of human Good,
Should acting, die, nor leave behind
Some lasting Pleasure in the Mind,
Which by Remembrance will assuage,

Grief, Sickness, Poverty, and Age;
And strongly shoot a radiant Dart,
To shine through Life's declining Part.

Say, *Stella*, feel you no Content,
Reflecting on a Life well spent?
Your skilful Hand employ'd to save
Despairing Wretches from the Grave;
And then supporting with your Store,
Those whom you dragg'd from Death before:
(So Providence on Mortals waits,
Preserving what it first creates)
Your gen'rous Boldness to defend
An innocent and absent Friend;
That Courage which can make you just,
To Merit humbled in the Dust:
The Detestation you express
For Vice in all its glitt'ring Dress:
That Patience under tort'ring Pain,
Where stubborn Stoicks would complain.

Shall these like empty Shadows pass,
Or Forms reflected from a Glass?
Or mere Chimæra's in the Mind,
That fly and leave no Marks behind?
Does not the Body thrive and grow
By Food of twenty Years ago?
And, had it not been still supply'd,
It must a thousand Times have dy'd.
Then, who with Reason can maintain,
That no Effects of Food remain?
And, is not Virtue in Mankind
The Nutriment that feeds the Mind?
Upheld by each good Action past,
And still continued by the last:
Then, who with Reason can pretend,
That all Effects of Virtue end?

Believe me *Stella*, when you show
That true Contempt for Things below,
Nor prize your Life for other Ends
Than merely to oblige your Friends;
Your former Actions claim their Part,
And join to fortify your Heart.
For Virtue in her daily Race,
Like *Janus*, bears a double Face;
Looks back with Joy where she has gone,
And therefore goes with Courage on.
She at your sickly Couch will wait,
And guide you to a better State.

O then, whatever Heav'n intends,
Take Pity on your pitying Friends;
Nor let your Ills affect your Mind,
To fancy they can be unkind.
Me, surely me, you ought to spare,
Who gladly would your Suff'rings share;
Or give my Scrap of Life to you,
And think it far beneath your Due;
You, to whose Care so oft I owe,
That I'm alive to tell you so.

Clever Tom Clinch going to be hanged

Written in the Year 1726

As clever *Tom Clinch*, while the Rabble was bawling,
Rode stately through *Holbourn*, to die in his Calling;
He stopt at the *George* for a Bottle of Sack,
And promis'd to pay for it when he'd come back.
His Waistcoat and Stockings, and Breeches were white,
His cap had a new Cherry Ribbon to ty't.
The Maids to the Doors and the Balconies ran,
And said, lack-a-day! he's a proper young Man.
But, as from the Windows the Ladies he spy'd,
Like a Beau in the Box, he bow'd low on each Side;
And when his last Speech the loud Hawkers did cry,
He swore from his Cart, it was all a damn'd Lye.
The Hangman for Pardon fell down on his Knee;
Tom gave him a Kick in the Guts for his Fee.
Then said, I must speak to the People a little,
But I'll see you all damn'd before I will *whittle*.
My honest Friend *Wild*, may he long hold his Place,
He lengthen'd my Life with a whole Year of Grace.
Take Courage, dear Comrades, and be not afraid,
Nor slip this Occasion to follow your Trade.
My Conscience is clear, and my Spirits are calm,
And thus I go off without Pray'r-Book or Psalm.
Then follow the Practice of clever *Tom Clinch*,
Who hung like a Hero, and never would flinch.

proper, handsome; *box*, at a theatre; *whittle*, confess; *Wild*, Jonathan Wild,
highwayman; *slip*, miss.

Holyhead. Sept. 25, 1727

Lo here I sit at holy head
With muddy ale and mouldy bread
All Christian vittals stink of fish
I'm where my enemyes would wish
Convict of lyes is every sign,
The Inn has not one drop of wine
I'm fasnd both by wind and tide
I see the ship at anchor ride
The Captain swears the sea's too rough
He has not passengers enough.
And thus the Dean is forc't to stay
Till others come to help the pay
In Dublin they'd be glad to see
A packet though it brings in me.
They cannot say the winds are cross
Your Politicians at a loss
For want of matter swears and fretts,
Are forced to read the old gazettes.
I never was in hast before
To reach that slavish hateful shore
Before, I always found the wind
To me was most malicious kind
But now, the danger of a friend
On whom my fears and hopes depend
Absent from whom all Clymes are curst
With whom I'm happy in the worst
With rage impatient makes me wait
A passage to the land I hate.
Else, rather on this bleaky shore
Where loudest winds incessant roar
Where neither herb nor tree will thrive,

Where nature hardly seems alive,
I'd go in freedom to my grave,
Than Rule yon Isle and be a Slave.

convict, guilty; *packet*, mail-boat; *a friend*, Stella; *yon isle*, Ireland.

Lady Acheson Weary of the Dean

I

The Dean wou'd visit Market-hill,
    Our Invitation was but slight
I said – why – Let him if he will,
    And so I bid Sir *Arthur* write.

II

His Manners would not let him wait,
    Least we should think ourselves neglected,
And so we saw him at our Gate
    Three Days before he was expected.

III

After a Week, a Month, a Quarter,
    And Day succeeding after Day,
Says not a Word of his Departure
    Tho' not a Soul would have him stay.

IV

I've said enough to make him blush
    Methinks, or else the Devil's in't,
But he cares not for it a Rush,
    Nor for my Life will take the Hint.

V

But you, my Life, may let him know,
    In civil Language, if he stays
How deep and foul the Roads may grow,
    And that he may command the Chaise.

VI

Or you may say – my Wife intends,
  Tho' I should be exceeding proud,
This Winter to invite some Friends,
  And Sir I know you hate a Crowd.

VII

Or, Mr. Dean – I should with Joy
  Beg you would here continue still,
But we must go to *Aghnacloy*;
  Or Mr. *Moor* will take it ill.

VIII

The House Accounts are daily rising
  So much his Stay do's swell the Bills;
My dearest Life it is surprizing,
  How much he eats, how much he swills.

IX

His Brace of Puppies how they stuff,
  And they must have three Meals a Day,
Yet never think they get enough;
  His Horses too eat all our Hay.

X

Oh! if I could, how I would maul
  His Tallow Face and Wainscot Paws,
His Beetle-brows and Eyes of Wall,
  And make him soon give up the Cause.

XI

Must I be every Moment chid
  With skinny, boney, snip and lean,

Oh! that I could but once be rid
    Of that insulting Tyrant Dean.

Drapier's Hill

We give the World to understand,
Our thriving Dean has purchas'd Land;
A Purchase which will bring him clear,
Above his Rent four Pounds a Year;
Provided, to improve the Ground,
He will but add two Hundred Pound,
And from his endless hoarded Store,
To build a House five Hundred more.
Sir *Arthur* too shall have his Will,
And call the Mansion *Drapier*'s Hill;
That when a Nation long enslav'd,
Forgets by whom it once was sav'd;
When none the Drapier's Praise shall sing;
His Signs aloft no longer swing;
His Medals and his Prints forgotten,
And all his Handkerchiefs are rotten;
His famous Letters made waste Paper;
This Hill may keep the Name of Drapier:
In Spight of Envy flourish still,
And Drapier's vye with Cooper's Hill.

Cooper's Hill; poem by Denham.

On burning a dull Poem
Written in the Year 1729

An Ass's Hoof alone can hold
That pois'nous Juice which kills by Cold.
Methought, when I this Poem read,
No Vessel but an Ass's Head,
Such frigid Fustian could contain;
I mean the Head without the Brain.
The cold Conceits, the chilling Thoughts,
Went down like stupifying Draughts:
I found my Head began to swim,
A Numbness crept through ev'ry Limb:
In Haste, with Imprecations dire,
I threw the Volume in the Fire:
When, who could think, tho' cold as Ice,
It burnt to Ashes in a Trice.

How could I more enhaunce it's Fame?
Though born in Snow, it dy'd in Flame.

On the Irish-Club

Ye paultry underlings of state,
Ye senators, who love to prate;
Ye rascals of inferior note,
Who, for a dinner, sell a vote;
Ye pack of pensionary Peers,
Whose fingers itch for poets ears;
Ye bishops far remov'd from saints;
Why all this rage? Why these complaints?
Why against Printers all this noise?
This summoning of blackguard boys?
Why so sagacious in your guesses?
Your *effs* and *tees*, and *arrs*, and *esses*?
Take my advice; to make you safe,
I know a shorter way by half.
The point is plain: Remove the cause;
Defend your liberties and laws.
Be sometimes to your country true,
Have once the public good in view:
Bravely despise Champagne at Court,
And chuse to dine at home with Port:
Let Prelates, by their good behaviour,
Convince us they believe a Saviour;
Nor sell what they so dearly bought,
This country, now their own, for nought.
Ne'er did a true satyric muse
Virtue or innocence abuse;
And 'tis against poetic rules
To rail at men by nature fools:
But * * * * * * * * *
* * * * * * * * * * *

Daphne

Daphne knows, with equal ease,
How to vex and how to please;
But, the folly of her sex
Makes her sole delight to vex.
Never woman more devis'd
Surer ways to be despis'd:
Paradoxes weakly wielding,
Always conquer'd, never yielding.
To dispute, her chief delight,
With not one opinion right:
Thick her arguments she lays on,
And with cavils combats reason:
Answers in decisive way,
Never hears what you can say:
Still her odd perverseness shows
Chiefly where she nothing knows.
And where she is most familiar,
Always peevisher and sillier:
All her spirits in a flame
When she knows she's most to blame.

   Send me hence ten thousand miles,
From a face that always smiles:
None could ever act that part,
But a Fury in her heart.
Ye who hate such inconsistence,
To be easy keep your distance;
Or in folly still befriend her,
But have no concern to mend her.
Lose not time to contradict her,
Nor endeavour to convict her.
Never take it in your thought,
That she'll own, or cure a fault.

Into contradiction warm her,
Then, perhaps, you may reform her:
Only take this rule along,
Always to advise her wrong;
And reprove her when she's right;
She may then grow wise for spight.

No – that scheme will ne'er succeed,
She has better learnt her creed:
She's too cunning, and too skilful,
When to yield, and when be willful.
Nature holds her forth two mirrors,
One for truth, and one for errors:
That looks hideous, fierce, and frightful;
This is flatt'ring, and delightful;
That she throws away as foul;
Sits by this, to dress her soul.

Thus you have the case in view,
Daphne, 'twixt the Dean and you,
Heav'n forbid he should despise thee;
But will never more advise thee.

TWELVE ARTICLES

1. Lest it may more quarrels breed
   I will never hear you read.
2. By disputing I will never
   To convince you, once endeavour.
3. When a paradox you stick to,
   I will never contradict you.
4. When I talk, and you are heedless,
   I will shew no anger needless.
5. When your speeches are absurd,
   I will ne'er object a word.
6. When you furious argue wrong,
   I will grieve, and hold my tongue.
7. Not a jest, or hum'rous story,

Will I ever tell before ye:
To be chidden for explaining
When you quite mistake the meaning.

8. Never more will I suppose
   You can taste my verse or prose:

9. You no more at me shall fret,
   While I teach, and you forget;

10. You shall never hear me thunder,
    When you blunder on, and blunder.

11. Shew your poverty of spirit,
    And in dress place all your merit;
    Give yourself ten thousand airs
    That with me shall break no squares.

12. Never will I give advice
    Till you please to ask me thrice;
    Which, if you in scorn reject,
    'Twill be just as I expect.

Thus we both shall have our ends,
And continue special friends.

The Dean to himself on St Cecilia's day

Grave D. of St Patrick's how comes it to pass
That you who know musick no more than an ass
That you who was found writing of Drapiers
Should lend your cathedral to players and scrapers
To act such an opera once in a year
Is offensive to every true Protestant ear
With trumpets and fiddles and organs and singing
Will sure the Pretend^r and Popery bring in.
No Protestant Prelate, His L^{d}shp or Grace
Durst there show his right or most revnd face
How would it pollute their Crosiers and Rochets
To listen to minimms and quavers and Crochets.

Rochets, surplices.

An Excellent New Ballad

or, The true English *Dean to be hang'd for a Rape*

I

Our Brethren of *England* who love us so dear,
And in all they do for us so kindly do mean,
A Blessing upon them, have sent us this Year,
For the Good of our Church a true *English* Dean.
    A holier Priest ne'er was wrapt up in Crape,
The worst you can say, he committed a Rape.

II

In his Journey to *Dublin*, he lighted at *Chester*,
And there he grew fond of another Man's Wife,
Burst into her Chamber, and wou'd have Carest her,
But she valu'd her Honour much more than her Life.
    She bustled and strugled, and made her Escape,
To a Room full of Guests for fear of a Rape.

III

The *Dean* he pursu'd to recover his Game,
And now to attack her again he prepares,
But the Company stood in Defence of the Dame,
They Cudgell'd, and Cuft him, and kickt him down Stairs.
    His Deanship was now in a damnable Scrape,
And this was no Time for committing a Rape.

IV

To *Dublin* he comes, to the *Bagnio* he goes,
And orders the Landlord to bring him a Whore;
No Scruple came on him his Gown to expose,
'Twas what all his Life he had practis'd before.
    He had made himself Drunk with the Juice of the Grape,
And got a good *Clap*, but committed no Rape.

V

The Dean, and his Landlord, a jolly Comrade,
Resolv'd for a Fortnight to Swim in Delight,
For why, they had both been brought up to the Trade
Of drinking all Day, and of whoring all Night.
His Landlord was ready his Deanship to Ape
In ev'ry Debauch, but committing a Rape.

VI

This *Protestant* Zealot, this *English* Divine
In Church and in State was of Principles sound,
Was truer than *Steel* to the *Hanover* Line,
And griev'd that a *Tory* should live above Ground.
Shall a Subject so Loyal be hang'd by the Nape,
For no other Crime but committing a Rape.

VII

By old *Popish* Cannons, as wise Men have Penn'd 'em,
Each Priest had a Concubine, *jure Ecclesiæ*;
Who'd be Dean of *Ferns* without a *Commendam*?
And Precedents we can produce, if it please ye,
Then, why should the Dean, when Whores are so cheap,
Be put to the Peril, and Toyl of a Rape?

VIII

If Fortune should please but to take such a Crotchet,
(To thee I apply great *Smedley*'s Successor)
To give thee *Lawn-Sleeves* a *Mitre* and *Rotchet*,
Whom would't thou resemble? I leave thee a Guesser;
But I only behold thee in *Atherton*'s Shape,
For *Sodomy* hang'd, as thou for a Rape.

IX

Ah! dost thou not Envy the brave Colonel *Chartres*,
Condemn'd for thy Crime, at three score and ten?
To Hang him all *England* would lend him their Garters;
Yet he lives,and is ready to ravish agen,
    Then Throttle thy self with an Ell of strong Tape,
For thou hast not a Groat to Attone for a Rape.

X

The Dean he was vext that his Whores were so willing,
He long'd for a Girl that would struggle and squal,
He ravish'd her fairly, and sav'd a good Shilling;
But, here was to pay the Devil and all.
    His Trouble and Sorrows now come in a Heap,
And hang'd he must be for committing a Rape.

XI

If Maidens are ravish't, it is their own Choice,
Why are they so willful to struggle with Men?
If they would but lye quiet, and stifle their Voice,
No Devil nor Dean could Ravish 'em then,
    Nor would there be need of a strong Hempen Cape,
Ty'd round the Dean's Neck, for committing a Rape.

XII

Our Church and our State dear *England* maintains,
For which all true Protestant Hearts should be glad;
She sends us our Bishops and Judges and Deans,
And better would give us, if better she had;
    But, Lord how the Rabble will stare and will gape,
When the good *English* Dean is hang'd up for a Rape.

The Lady's Dressing Room

Five Hours, (and who can do it less in?)
By haughty *Celia* spent in Dressing;
The Goddess from her Chamber issues,
Array'd in Lace, Brocade and Tissues.
Strephon, who found the Room was void,
And *Betty* otherwise employ'd;
Stole in, and took a strict Survey,
Of all the Litter as it lay;
Whereof, to make the Matter clear,
An Inventory follows here.

And first a dirty Smock appear'd,
Beneath the Arm-pits well besmear'd.
Strephon, the Rogue, display'd it wide,
And turn'd it round on every Side.
In such a Case few Words are best,
And *Strephon* bids us guess the rest;
But swears how damnably the Men lie,
In calling *Celia* sweet and cleanly.

Now listen while he next produces,
The various Combs for various Uses,
Fill'd up with Dirt so closely fixt,
No Brush could force a way betwixt.
A Paste of Composition rare,
Sweat, Dandriff, Powder, Lead and Hair;
A Forehead Cloth with Oyl upon't
To smooth the Wrinkles on her Front;
Here Allum Flower to stop the Steams,
Exhal'd from sour unsavoury Streams,
There Night-gloves made of *Tripsy*'s Hide,
Bequeath'd by *Tripsy* when she dy'd,
With Puppy Water, Beauty's Help
Distill'd from *Tripsy*'s darling Whelp;

Here Gallypots and Vials plac'd,
Some fill'd with Washes, some with Paste,
Some with Pomatum, Paints and Slops,
And Ointments good for scabby Chops.
Hard by a filthy Bason stands,
Fowl'd with the Scouring of her Hands;
The Bason takes whatever comes
The Scrapings of her Teeth and Gums,
A nasty Compound of all Hues,
For here she spits, and here she spues.

But oh! it turn'd poor *Strephon*'s Bowels,
When he beheld and smelt the Towels,
Begumm'd, bematter'd, and beslim'd
With Dirt, and Sweat, and Ear-Wax grim'd.
No Object *Strephon*'s Eye escapes,
Here Pettycoats in frowzy Heaps;
Nor be the Handkerchiefs forgot
All varnish'd o'er with Snuff and Snot.
The Stockings, why shou'd I expose,
Stain'd with the Marks of stinking Toes;
Or greasy Coifs and Pinners reeking,
Which *Celia* slept at least a Week in?
A Pair of Tweezers next he found
To pluck her Brows in Arches round,
Or Hairs that sink the Forehead low,
Or on her Chin like Bristles grow.

The Virtues we must not let pass,
Of *Celia*'s magnifying Glass.
When frighted *Strephon* cast his Eye on't
It shew'd the Visage of a Gyant.
A Glass that can to Sight disclose,
The smallest Worm in *Celia*'s Nose,
And faithfully direct her Nail
To squeeze it out from Head to Tail;
For catch it nicely by the Head,
It must come out alive or dead.

Why *Strephon* will you tell the rest?
And must you needs describe the Chest?
That careless Wench! no Creature warn her
To move it out from yonder Corner;
But leave it standing full in Sight
For you to exercise your Spight.
In vain, the Workman shew'd his Wit
With Rings and Hinges counterfeit
To make it seem in this Disguise,
A Cabinet to vulgar Eyes;
Which *Strephon* ventur'd to look in,
Resolv'd to go thro' thick and thin;
He lifts the Lid, there need no more,
He smelt it all the Time before.
As from within *Pandora*'s Box,
When *Epimetheus* op'd the Locks,
A sudden universal Crew
Of humane Evils upward flew;
He still was comforted to find
That *Hope* at last remain'd behind;
So *Strephon* lifting up the Lid,
To view what in the Chest was hid,
The Vapours flew from out the Vent,
But *Strephon* cautious never meant
The Bottom of the Pan to grope,
And fowl his Hands in Search of *Hope*.
O ne'er may such a vile Machine
Be once in *Celia*'s Chamber seen!
O may she better learn to keep
'Those Secrets of the hoary deep!'

As Mutton Cutlets, Prime of Meat,
Which tho' with Art you salt and beat,
As Laws of Cookery require,
And roast them at the clearest Fire;
If from adown the hopeful Chops

The Fat upon a Cinder drops,
To stinking Smoak it turns the Flame
Pois'ning the Flesh from whence it came;
And up exhales a greasy Stench,
For which you curse the careless Wench;
So Things, which must not be exprest,
When plumpt into the reeking Chest;
Send up an excremental Smell
To taint the Parts from whence they fell.
The Pettycoats and Gown perfume,
And waft a Stink round every Room.

    Thus finishing his grand Survey,
The Swain disgusted slunk away. [. . .]

    But Vengeance, Goddess never sleeping
Soon punish'd *Strephon* for his Peeping;
His foul Imagination links
Each Dame he sees with all her Stinks:
And, if unsav'ry Odours fly,
Conceives a Lady standing by:
All Women his Description fits,
And both Idea's jump like Wits:
By vicious Fancy coupled fast,
And still appearing in Contrast.
I pity wretched *Strephon* blind
To all the Charms of Woman Kind;
Should I the Queen of Love refuse,
Because she rose from stinking Ooze?
To him that looks behind the Scene,
Satira's but some pocky Quean.

    When *Celia* in her Glory shows,
If *Strephon* would but stop his Nose;
(Who now so impiously blasphemes
Her Ointments, Daubs, and Paints and Creams,
Her Washes, Slops, and every Clout,

With which he makes so foul a Rout;)
He soon would learn to think like me,
And bless his ravisht Eyes to see
Such Order from Confusion sprung,
Such gaudy Tulips rais'd from Dung.

alum flower, *etc.*, cosmetics; *jump*, coincide

A Beautiful Young Nymph Going to Bed

Corinna, Pride of *Drury-Lane*,
For whom no Shepherd sighs in vain;
Never did *Covent Garden* boast
So bright a batter'd, strolling Toast;
No drunken Rake to pick her up,
No Cellar where on Tick to sup;
Returning at the Midnight Hour;
Four Stories climbing to her Bow'r;
Then, seated on a three-legg'd Chair,
Takes off her artificial Hair:
Now, picking out a Crystal Eye,
She wipes it clean, and lays it by.
Her Eye-Brows from a Mouse's Hyde,
Stuck on with Art on either Side,
Pulls off with Care, and first displays 'em,
Then in a Play-Book smoothly lays 'em.
Now dextrously her Plumpers draws,
That serve to fill her hollow Jaws.
Untwists a Wire; and from her Gums
A Set of Teeth completely comes.
Pulls out the Rags contriv'd to prop
Her flabby Dugs and down they drop.
Proceeding on, the lovely Goddess
Unlaces next her Steel-Rib'd Bodice;
Which by the Operator's Skill,
Press down the Lumps, the Hollows fill,
Up goes her Hand, and off she slips
The Bolsters that supply her Hips.
With gentlest Touch, she next explores
Her Shankers, Issues, running Sores,
Effects of many a sad Disaster;
And then to each applies a Plaister,
But must, before she goes to Bed,

Rub off the Dawbs of White and Red;
And smooth the Furrows in her Front,
With greasy Paper stuck upon't.
She takes a *Bolus* e'er she sleeps;
And then between two Blankets creeps.
With Pains of Love tormented lies;
Or if she chance to close her Eyes,
Of *Bridewell* and the *Compter* dreams,
And feels the Lash, and faintly screams;
Or, by a faithless Bully drawn,
At some Hedge-Tavern lies in Pawn;
Or to *Jamaica* seems transported,
Alone, and by no Planter courted;
Or, near *Fleet-Ditch*'s oozy brinks,
Surrounded with a Hundred Stinks,
Belated, seems on watch to lye,
And snap some Cully passing by;
Or, struck with Fear, her Fancy runs
On Watchmen, Constables and Duns,
From whom she meets with frequent Rubs;
But, never from Religious Clubs;
Whose Favour she is sure to find,
Because she pays them all in Kind.

   Corinna wakes. A dreadful Sight!
Behold the Ruins of the Night!
A wicked Rat her Plaister stole,
Half eat, and dragg'd it to his Hole.
The Crystal Eye, alas, was miss't;
And *Puss* had on her Plumpers pisst.
A Pigeon pick'd her Issue-Peas;
And *Shock* her Tresses fill'd with Fleas.

   THE Nymph, tho' in this mangled Plight,
Must ev'ry Morn her Limbs unite.
But how shall I describe her Arts
To recollect the scatter'd Parts?
Or shew the Anguish, Toil, and Pain,

Of gath'ring up herself again?
The bashful Muse will never bear
In such a Scene to interfere.
Corinna in the Morning dizen'd,
Who sees, will spew; who smells, be poison'd.

shankers, sores; *front*, forehead; *compter*, prison; *bully*, pimp; *rubs*,
confrontations; *religious clubs*, reformation groups; *issue-peas*, surgical
dressings.

Verses on the Death of Dr *Swift*, D.S.P.D.
Occasioned by reading a Maxim in Rochefoulcault

As *Rochefoucault* his Maxims drew
From Nature, I believe 'em true:
They argue no corrupted Mind
In him; the Fault is in Mankind.

This Maxim more than all the rest
Is thought too base for human Breast;
'In all Distresses of our Friends
'We first consult our private Ends,
'While Nature kindly bent to ease us,
'Points out some Circumstance to please us.'

If this perhaps your Patience move
Let Reason and Experience prove.

We all behold with envious Eyes,
Our *Equal* rais'd above our *Size*;
Who wou'd not at a crowded Show,
Stand high himself, keep others low?
I love my Friend as well as you,
But would not have him stop my View;
Then let me have the higher Post;
I ask but for an Inch at most.

If in a Battle you should find,
One, whom you love of all Mankind,
Had some heroick Action done,
A Champion kill'd, or Trophy won;
Rather than thus be over-topt,
Would you not wish his Lawrels cropt?

Dear honest *Ned* is in the Gout,
Lies rackt with Pain, and you without:
How patiently you hear him groan!
How glad the Case is not your own!

What Poet would not grieve to see,
His Brethren write as well as he?
But rather than they should excel,
He'd wish his Rivals all in Hell.

Her End when Emulation misses,
She turns to Envy, Stings and Hisses:
The strongest Friendship yields to Pride,
Unless the Odds be on our Side.

Vain human Kind! Fantastick Race!
Thy various Follies, who can trace?
Self-love, Ambition, Envy, Pride,
Their Empire in our Hearts divide:
Give others Riches, Power, and Station,
'Tis all on me an Usurpation.
I have no Title to aspire;
Yet, when you sink, I seem the higher.
In POPE, I cannot read a Line,
But with a Sigh, I wish it mine:
When he can in one Couplet fix
More Sense than I can do in Six:
It gives me such a jealous Fit,
I cry, Pox take him, and his Wit.
Why must I be outdone by GAY,
In my own hum'rous biting Way?

ARBUTHNOT is no more my Friend,
Who dares to Irony pretend;
Which I was born to introduce,
Refin'd it first, and shew'd its Use.

St John, as well as Pultney knows,
That I had some repute for Prose;
And till they drove me out of Date,
Could maul a Minister of State:
If they have mortify'd my Pride,
And made me throw my Pen aside;
If with such Talents Heav'n hath blest 'em
Have I not Reason to detest 'em?

To all my Foes, dear Fortune, send
Thy Gifts, but never to my Friend:
I tamely can endure the first,
But, this with Envy makes me burst.

Thus much may serve by way of Proem,
Proceed we therefore to our Poem.

The Time is not remote, when I
Must by the Course of Nature dye:
When I foresee my special Friends,
Will try to find their private Ends:
Tho' it is hardly understood,
Which way my Death can do them good;
Yet, thus methinks, I hear 'em speak;
See, how the Dean begins to break:
Poor Gentleman, he droops apace,
You plainly find it in his Face:
That old Vertigo in his Head,
Will never leave him, till he's dead:
Besides, his Memory decays,
He recollects not what he says;
He cannot call his Friends to Mind;
Forgets the Place where last he din'd:
Plyes you with Stories o'er and o'er,
He told them fifty Times before.
How does he fancy we can sit,
To hear his out-of-fashion'd Wit?

But he takes up with younger Fokes,
Who for his Wine will bear his Jokes:
Faith, he must make his Stories shorter,
Or change his Comrades once a Quarter:
In half the Time, he talks them round;
There must another Sett be found.

For Poetry, he's past his Prime,
He takes an Hour to find a Rhime:
His Fire is out, his Wit decay'd,
His Fancy sunk, his Muse a Jade.
I'd have him throw away his Pen;
But there's no talking to some Men.

And, then their Tenderness appears,
By adding largely to my Years:
'He's older than he would be reckon'd,
'And well remembers *Charles* the Second.

'He hardly drinks a Pint of Wine;
'And that, I doubt, is no good Sign.
'His Stomach too begins to fail:
'Last Year we thought him strong and hale;
'But now, he's quite another Thing;
'I wish he may hold out till Spring.'

Then hug themselves, and reason thus;
'It is not yet so bad with us.'

In such a Case they talk in Tropes,
And, by their Fears express their Hopes:
Some great Misfortune to portend,
No Enemy can match a Friend;
With all the Kindness they profess,
The Merit of a lucky Guess,
(When daily Howd'y's come of Course,
And Servants answer; *Worse and Worse*)
Wou'd please 'em better than to tell,

That, GOD be prais'd, the Dean is well.
Then he who prophecy'd the best,
Approves his Foresight to the rest:
'You know, I always fear'd the worst,
'And often told you so at first:'
He'd rather chuse that I should dye,
Than his Prediction prove a Lye.
Not one foretels I should recover;
But, all agree, to give me over.

Yet shou'd some Neighbour feel a Pain,
Just in the Parts, where I complain;
How many a Message would he send?
What hearty Prayers that I should mend?
Enquire what Regimen I kept;
What gave me Ease, and how I slept?
And more lament, when I was dead,
Than all the Sniv'llers round my Bed.

My good Companions, never fear,
For though you may mistake a Year;
Though your Prognosticks run too fast,
They must be verify'd at last.

'Behold the fatal Day arrive!
'How is the Dean? He's just alive.
'Now the departing Prayer is read:
'He hardly breathes. The Dean is dead.
'Before the Passing-Bell begun,
'The News thro' half the Town has run.
'O, may we all for Death prepare!
'What has he left? And who's his Heir?
'I know no more than what the News is,
'Tis all bequeath'd to publick Uses.
'To publick Use! A perfect Whim!
'What had the Publick done for him!
'Meer Envy, Avarice, and Pride!

'He gave it all: – But first he dy'd.
'And had the Dean, in all the Nation,
'No worthy Friend, no poor Relation?
'So ready to do Strangers good,
'Forgetting his own Flesh and Blood?'

Now Grub-Street Wits are all employ'd;
With Elegies, the Town is cloy'd:
Some Paragraph in ev'ry Paper,
To *curse* the *Dean*, or *bless* the *Drapier*.

The Doctors tender of their Fame,
Wisely on me lay all the Blame:
'We must confess his Case was nice;
'But he would never take Advice:
'Had he been rul'd, for ought appears,
'He might have liv'd these Twenty Years:
'For when we open'd him we found,
'That all his vital Parts were sound.'

From *Dublin* soon to *London* spread,
'Tis told at Court, the Dean is dead.

Kind Lady *Suffolk* in the Spleen,
Runs laughing up to tell the Queen.
The Queen, so Gracious, Mild, and Good,
Cries, 'Is he gone? 'Tis time he shou'd.
'He's dead you say; why let him rot;
'I'm glad the Medals were forgot.
'I promis'd them, I own; but when?
'I only was the Princess then;
'But now as Consort of the King,
'You know 'tis quite a different Thing.'

Now, *Chartres* at Sir *Robert*'s Levee,
Tells, with a Sneer, the Tidings heavy:
'Why, is he dead without his Shoes?'
(Cries *Bob*) 'I'm Sorry for the News;

'Oh, were the Wretch but living still,
'And in his Place my good Friend *Will*;
'Or, had a Mitre on his Head
'Provided *Bolingbroke* were dead.'

Now *Curl* his Shop from Rubbish drains;
Three genuine Tomes of *Swift*'s Remains.
And then to make them pass the glibber,
Revis'd by *Tibbalds, Moore, and Cibber.*
He'll treat me as he does my Betters.
Publish my Will, my Life, my Letters.
Revive the Libels born to dye;
Which POPE must bear, as well as I.

Here shift the Scene, to represent
How those I love, my Death lament.
Poor POPE will grieve a Month; and GAY
A Week; and ARBUTHNOTT a Day.

ST JOHN himself will scarce forbear,
To bite his Pen, and drop a Tear.
The rest will give a Shrug and cry
I'm sorry; but we all must dye.
Indifference clad in Wisdom's Guise,
All Fortitude of Mind supplies:
For how can stony Bowels melt,
In those who never Pity felt;
When *We* are lash'd, *They* kiss the Rod;
Resigning to the Will of God.

The Fools, my Juniors by a Year,
Are tortur'd with Suspence and Fear.
Who wisely thought my Age a Screen,
When Death approach'd, to stand between:
The Screen remov'd, their Hearts are trembling,
They mourn for me without dissembling.

My female Friends, whose tender Hearts
Have better learn'd to act their parts,
Receive the News in *doleful Dumps,*
'The Dean is dead, (*and what is Trumps?*)
'Then Lord have Mercy on his Soul.
'(Ladies I'll venture for the *Vole.*)
'Six Deans they say must bear the Pall.
'(I wish I knew what *King* to call.)
'Madam, your Husband will attend
'The Funeral of so good a Friend.
'No Madam, 'tis a shocking Sight,
'And he's engag'd To-morrow Night!
'My Lady *Club* wou'd take it ill,
'If he shou'd fail her at *Quadrill.*
'He lov'd the Dean. (*I lead a Heart.*)
'But dearest Friends, they say, must part.
'His Time was come, he ran his Race;
'We hope he's in a better Place.'

Why do we grieve that Friends should dye?
No loss more easy to supply.
One Year is past; a different Scene;
No further mention of the Dean;
Who now, alas, no more is mist,
Than if he never did exist.
Where's now this Fav'rite of *Apollo?*
Departed; *and his Works must follow:*
Must undergo the common Fate;
His Kind of Wit is out of Date.
Some Country Squire to *Lintot* goes,
Enquires for SWIFT in Verse and Prose:
Says *Lintot,* 'I have heard the Name:
'He dy'd a Year ago.' The same.
He searcheth all his Shop in vain;
'Sir you may find them in *Duck-lane*:

'I sent them with a Load of Books,
'Last *Monday* to the Pastry-cooks.
'To fancy they cou'd live a Year!
'I find you're but a Stranger here.
'The Dean was famous in his Time;
'And had a Kind of Knack at Rhyme:
'His way of Writing now is past;
'The Town hath got a better Taste:
'I keep no antiquated Stuff;
'But, spick and span I have enough.
'Pray, do but give me leave to shew 'em;
'Here's *Colley Cibber*'s Birth-day Poem.
'This Ode you never yet have seen,
'By *Stephen Duck*, upon the Queen.
'Then, here's a Letter finely penn'd
'Against the *Craftsman* and his Friend;
'It clearly shews that all Reflection
'On Ministers, is disaffection.
'Next, here's Sir *Robert*'s Vindication,
'And Mr. *Henly*'s last Oration:
'The Hawkers have not got 'em yet,
'Your Honour please to buy a Set?

'Here's Wolston's Tracts, the twelfth Edition;
' 'Tis read by ev'ry Politician:
'The Country Members, when in Town,
'To all their Boroughs send them down:
'You never met a Thing so smart;
'The Courtiers have them all by Heart:
'Those Maids of Honour (who can read)
'Are taught to use them for their Creed.
'The Rev'rend Author's good Intention,
'Hath been rewarded with a Pension:
'He doth an Honour to his Gown,
'By bravely running *Priest-craft* down:
'He shews, as sure as GOD's in *Gloc'ster*,

'That *Jesus* was a Grand Impostor:
'That all his Miracles were Cheats,
'Perform'd as Juglers do their Feats:
'The Church had never such a Writer:
'A Shame, he hath not got a Mitre!'

    Suppose me dead; and then suppose
A Club assembled at the *Rose*;
Where from Discourse of this and that,
I grow the Subject of their Chat:
And, while they toss my Name about,
With Favour some, and some without;
One quite indiff'rent in the Cause,
My Character impartial draws:

    'The Dean, if we believe Report,
'Was never ill receiv'd at Court:
'As for his Works in Verse and Prose,
'I own my self no Judge of those:
'Nor, can I tell what Criticks thought 'em;
'But, this I know, all People bought 'em;
'As with a moral View design'd
'To cure the Vices of Mankind:
'His Vein, ironically grave,
'Expos'd the Fool, and lash'd the Knave:
'To steal a Hint was never known,
'But what he writ was all his own.

    'He never thought an Honour done him,
'Because a Duke was proud to own him:
'Would rather slip aside, and chuse
'To talk with Wits in dirty Shoes:
'Despis'd the Fools with Stars and Garters,
'So often seen caressing *Chartres*:
'He never courted Men in Station,
'*Nor Persons had in Admiration*;
'Of no Man's Greatness was afraid,

84

'Because he sought for no Man's Aid.
'Though trusted long in great Affairs,
'He gave himself no haughty Airs:
'Without regarding private Ends,
'Spent all his Credit for his Friends:
'And only chose the Wise and Good;
'No Flatt'rers; no Allies in Blood;
'But succour'd Virtue in Distress,
'And seldom fail'd of good Success;
'As Numbers in their Hearts must own,
'Who, but for him, had been unknown.

'With Princes kept a due Decorum,
'But never stood in Awe before 'em:
And to her Majesty, God bless her,
'Would speak as free as to her Dresser,
'She thought it his peculiar Whim,
'Nor took it ill as come from him.
'He follow'd *David*'s Lesson just,
'*In Princes never put thy Trust.*
'And, would you make him truly sower;
Provoke him with *a slave in Power*:
'The *Irish* Senate, if you nam'd,
'With what Impatience he declaim'd!
'Fair LIBERTY was all his Cry;
'For her he stood prepar'd to die;
'For her he boldly stood alone;
'For her he oft expos'd his own.
'Two Kingdoms, just as Faction led,
'Had set a Price upon his Head;
'But, not a Traytor cou'd be found,
'To sell him for Six Hundred Pound.

'Had he but spar'd his Tongue and Pen,
'He might have rose like other Men:
'But, Power was never in his Thought;
'And, Wealth he valu'd not a Groat:

'Ingratitude he often found,
'And pity'd those who meant the Wound:
'But, kept the Tenor of his Mind,
'To merit well of human Kind:
'Nor made a Sacrifice of those
'Who still were true, to please his Foes.
'He labour'd many a fruitless Hour
'To reconcile his Friends in Power;
'Saw Mischief by a Faction brewing,
'While they pursu'd each others Ruin.
'But, finding vain was all his Care,
'He left the Court in meer Despair.

    'And, oh! how short are human Schemes!
'Here ended all our golden Dreams.
'What ST JOHN's Skill in State Affairs,
'What ORMOND's *Valour*, OXFORD's Cares,
'To save their sinking Country lent,
'Was all destroy'd by one Event.
'Too soon that precious Life was ended,
'On which alone, our Weal depended.
'When up a dangerous Faction starts,
'With Wrath and Vengeance in their Hearts:
'*By solemn League and Cov'nant bound*,
'To ruin, slaughter, and confound;
'To turn Religion to a Fable,
'And make the Government a *Babel*:
'Pervert the Law, disgrace the Gown,
'Corrupt the Senate, rob the Crown;
'To sacrifice old *England*'s Glory,
'And make her infamous in Story.
'When such a Tempest shook the Land,
'How could unguarded Virtue stand?

    'With Horror, Grief, Despair the Dean
'Beheld the dire destructive Scene:
'His Friends in Exile, or the Tower,

'Himself within the Frown of Power;
'Pursu'd by base envenom'd Pens,
'Far to the Land of Slaves and Fens;
'A servile Race in Folly nurs'd,
'Who truckle most, when treated worst.

    'By Innocence and Resolution,
'He bore continual Persecution;
'While Numbers to Preferment rose;
'Whose Merits were, to be his Foes.
'When, *ev'n his own familiar Friends*
'Intent upon their private Ends;
'Like Renegadoes now he feels,
'*Against him lifting up their Heels.*

    'The Dean did by his Pen defeat
'An infamous destructive Cheat.
'Taught Fools their Int'rest how to know;
'And gave them Arms to ward the Blow.
'Envy hath own'd it was his doing,
'To save that helpless Land from Ruin,
'While they who at the Steerage stood,
'And reapt the Profit, sought his Blood.

    'To save them from their evil Fate,
'In him was held a Crime of State.
'A wicked Monster on the Bench,
'Whose Fury Blood could never quench;
'As vile and profligate a Villain,
'As modern *Scroggs*, or old *Tressilian*;
'Who long all Justice had discarded,
'*Nor fear'd he GOD, nor Man regarded;*
'Vow'd on the Dean his Rage to vent,
'And make him of his Zeal repent;
'But Heav'n his Innocence defends,
'The grateful People stand his Friends:
'Not Strains of Law, nor Judges Frown,

'Nor Topicks brought to please the Crown,
'Nor Witness hir'd, nor Jury pick'd,
'Prevail to bring him in convict.

   'In Exile with a steady Heart,
'He spent his Life's declining Part;
'Where, Folly, Pride, and Faction sway,
'Remote from St John, Pope, and Gay.

   'His Friendship there to few confin'd,
'Were always of the midling Kind:
'No Fools of Rank, a mungril Breed,
'Who fain would pass for Lords indeed:
'Where Titles give no Right or Power,
'And Peerage is a wither'd Flower,
'He would have held it a Disgrace,
'If such a Wretch had known his Face.
'On Rural Squires, that Kingdom's Bane,
'He vented oft his Wrath in vain:
'Biennial Squires, to Market brought;
'Who sell their Souls and Votes for Naught;
'The Nation stript go joyful back,
'To rob the Church, their Tenants rack,
'Go Snacks with Thieves and Rapparees,
'And, keep the Peace, to pick up Fees:
'In every Jobb to have a Share,
'A Jayl or Barrack to repair;
'And turn the Tax for publick Roads
'Commodious to their own Abodes.

   'Perhaps I may allow, the Dean
'Had too much Satyr in his Vein;
'And seem'd determin'd not to starve it,
'Because no Age could more deserve it.
'Yet, Malice never was his Aim;
'He lash'd the Vice but spar'd the Name.
'No Individual could resent,

'Where Thousands equally were meant.
'His Satyr points at no Defect,
'But what all Mortals may correct;
'For he abhorr'd that senseless Tribe,
'Who call it Humour when they jibe:
'He spar'd a Hump or crooked Nose,
'Whose Owners set not up for Beaux.
'True genuine Dulness mov'd his Pity,
'Unless it offer'd to be witty.
'Those, who their Ignorance confess'd,
'He ne'er offended with a Jest;
'But laugh'd to hear an Idiot quote,
'A Verse from *Horace*, learn'd by Rote.

   'He knew an hundred pleasant Stories,
'With all the Turns of *Whigs* and *Tories*:
'Was chearful to his dying Day,
'And Friends would let him have his Way.

   'He gave the little Wealth he had,
'To build a House for Fools and Mad:
'And shew'd by one satyric Touch,
'No Nation wanted it so much:
'That Kingdom he hath left his Debtor,
'I wish it soon may have a Better.'

D.S.P.D., Dean of St. Patrick's, Dublin; *move*, try; *break*, fail; *without his shoes*,
not hanged; *vertigo*, stress on second syllable; *talks them round*, tells them all;
stomach, appetite; *approves*, demonstrates; *wisely*, sagely; *vole*, a win at
quadrille; *Craftsman*, a Tory paper; *pastry-cook's*, as wrapping; *mere*, utter;
snacks, shares; *rapparees*, Irish highwaymen; *keep the peace*, act as magistrates;
job, scheme, racket.

Helter Skelter
or, The Hue and Cry after the Attornies,
going to ride the Circuit

Now the active young Attornies
Briskly travel on their Journies,
Looking big as any Gyants,
On the Horses of their Clients;
Like so many little Mars's,
With their Tilters at their Arses,
Brazen hilted lately burnish'd,
And with Harness-Buckles furnish'd;
And with Whips and Spurs so neat,
And with Jockey-Coats compleat;
And with Boots so very grazy
And with Saddles eke so easy
And with Bridles fine and gay,
Bridles borrow'd for a Day,
Bridles destin'd far to roam,
Ah! never to return Home;
And with Hats so very big, Sir,
And wi[t]h powder'd Caps and Wigs, Sir;
And with Ruffles to be shewn,
Cambrick Ruffles not their own;
And with Holland Shirts so white,
Shirts becoming to the sight,
Shirts be wrought with different Letters,
As belonging to their betters:
With their pretty tinsel'd Boxes,
Gotten from their dainty Doxies,
And with Rings so very trim,
Lately taken out of Lim –
And with very little Pence,
And as very little Sence:
With some Law but little Justice,

Having stolen from mine Hostess,
From the Barber and the Cutler,
Like the Soldier from the Sutler;
From the Vintner and the Taylor,
Like the Felon from the Jailer,
Into this and t'other County,
Living on the publick Bounty;
Thorough Town and thorough Village,
All to plunder, all to pillage;
Thorow Mountains thorow Vallies;
Thorow stinking Lanes and Allies;
Some to Cuckold Farmers Spouses
And make merry in their Houses;
Some to tumble Country-Wenches
On their Rushy Beds and Benches,
And, if they begin a Fray,
Draw their Swords and run away:
All to murder Equity,
And to take a double Fee;
Till the People all are quiet
And forget to broil and riot,
Low in Pocket, Cow'd in Courage,
Safely glad to sup their Porridge,
And Vacation's over – then
Hey for Dublin Town agen!

tilters, swords; *letters*, monograms; *lim*, pawn.

Verses on I Know Not What

My latest tribute here I send
With this let your Collection end
Thus I consign you down to Fame,
A Character to praise and blame,
And, if the whole may pass for true,
Contented rest; you have your due
Give future times the Satisfaction
To leave one handle for Detraction.

'A Paper Book is sent by *Boyle*'

A Paper Book is sent by *Boyle*,
Too neatly guilt for me to soil.
Delany sends a Silver Standish,
When I no more a Pen can brandish.
Let both around my Tomb be plac'd,
As Trophies of a Muse deceas'd:
And let the friendly Lines they writ
In praise of long departed Wit,
Be grav'd on either Side in Columns,
More to my Praise than all my Volumes;
To burst with Envy, Spite, and Rage,
The *Vandals* of the present Age.

The Day of Judgement

With a Whirl of Thought oppress'd,
I sink from Reverie to Rest.
An horrid Vision seiz'd my Head,
I saw the Graves give up their Dead.
Jove, arm'd with Terrors, burst the Skies,
And Thunder roars, and Light'ning flies!
Amaz'd, confus'd, its Fate unknown,
The World stands trembling at his Throne.
While each pale Sinner hangs his Head,
Jove, nodding, shook the Heav'ns, and said,
'Offending Race of Human Kind,
By Nature, Reason, Learning, blind;
You who thro' Frailty step'd aside,
And you who never fell – *thro' Pride*;
You who in different Sects have shamm'd,
And come to see each other damn'd;
(So some Folks told you, but they knew
No more of Jove's Designs than you)
The World's mad Business now is o'er,
And I resent these Pranks no more.
I to such Blockheads set my Wit!
I damn such Fools! – Go, go, you're bit.'

from On Poetry: A Rapsody

All Human Race wou'd fain be *Wits*,
And Millions miss, for one that hits.
Young's universal Passion, *Pride*,
Was never known to spread so wide.
Say *Britain*, cou'd you ever boast, —
Three *Poets* in an Age at most?
Our chilling Climate hardly bears
A *Sprig* of Bays in Fifty Years:
While ev'ry Fool his Claim alledges,
As if it grew in common Hedges.
What Reason can there be assign'd
For this Perverseness in the Mind?
Brutes find out where their Talents lie:
A *Bear* will not attempt to fly:
A founder'd *Horse* will oft debate,
Before he tries a five-barr'd Gate:
A *Dog* by Instinct turns aside,
Who sees the Ditch too deep and wide,
But *Man* we find the only Creature,
Who, led by *Folly*, combats *Nature*;
Who, when *she* loudly cries, *Forbear*,
With Obstinacy fixes there;
And, where his *Genius* least inclines,
Absurdly bends his whole Designs.

Not *Empire* to the Rising-Sun,
By Valour, Conduct, Fortune won;
Nor highest *Wisdom* in Debates
For framing Laws to govern States;
Nor Skill in Sciences profound,
So large to grasp the Circle round;
Such heavenly Influence require,
As how to strike the *Muses Lyre*.

Not Beggar's Brat, on Bulk begot;
Not Bastard of a Pedlar *Scot*;
Not Boy brought up to cleaning Shoes,
The Spawn of *Bridewell*, or the Stews;
Not Infants dropt, the spurious Pledges
Of *Gipsies* littering under Hedges,
Are so disqualified by Fate
To rise in *Church*, or *Law*, or *State*,
As he, whom *Phebus* in his Ire
Hath *blasted* with poetick Fire.

What hope of Custom in the *Fair*,
While not a Soul demands your Ware?
Where you have nothing to produce
For private Life, or publick Use?
Court, *City*, *Country* want you not;
You cannot bribe, betray, or plot.
For Poets, Law makes no Provision:
The Wealthy have you in Derision.
Of State-Affairs you cannot smatter,
Are awkward when you try to flatter.

Your Portion, taking *Britain* round,
Was just one annual Hundred Pound.
Now not so much as in Remainder
Since *Cibber* brought in an Attainder;
For ever fixt by Right Divine,
(A Monarch's Right) on *Grubstreet* Line.
Poor starv'ling Bard, how small thy Gains!
How unproportion'd to thy Pains!

And here a *Simile* comes Pat in:
Tho' *Chickens* take a Month to fatten,
The Guests in less than half an Hour
Will more than half a Score devour.
So, after toiling twenty Days,
To earn a Stock of Pence and Praise,

Thy Labours, grown the Critick's Prey,
Are swallow'd o'er a Dish of Tea;
Gone, to be never heard of more,
Gone, where the *Chickens* went before.

How shall a new Attempter learn
Of diff'rent Spirits to discern,
And how distinguish, which is which,
The Poet's Vein, or scribling Itch?
Then hear an old experience'd Sinner
Instructing thus a young Beginner.

Consult yourself, and if you find
A powerful Impulse urge your Mind,
Impartial judge within your Breast
What Subject you can manage best;
Whether your Genius most inclines
To Satire, Praise, or hum'rous Lines;
To Elegies in mournful Tone,
Or Prologue sent from Hand unknown.
Then rising with *Aurora*'s Light,
The Muse invok'd, sit down to write;
Blot out, correct, insert, refine,
Enlarge, diminish, interline;
Be mindful, when Invention fails,
To scratch your Head, and bite yours Nails.

Your Poem finish'd, next your Care
Is needful, to transcribe it fair.
In modern Wit all printed Trash, is
Set off with num'rous *Breaks* — and *Dashes* –

To Statesmen wou'd you give a Wipe,
You print it in *Italick Type*,
When Letters are in vulgar Shapes,
'Tis ten to one the Wit escapes;
But then in *Capitals* exprest,
The dullest Reader smoaks a Jest:

Or else perhaps he may invent
A better than the Poet meant,
As learned Commentators view
In *Homer* more than *Homer* knew.

    Your Poem in its modish Dress,
Correctly fitted for the Press,
Convey by Penny-Post to *Lintot*,
But let no Friend alive look into't.
If *Lintot* thinks 'twil quit the Cost,
You need not fear your Labour lost:
And, how agreeably surpriz'd
Are you to see it advertiz'd!
The Hawker shews you one in Print,
As fresh as Farthings from the Mint:
The Product of your Toil and Sweating;
A Bastard of your own begetting.

    Be sure at *Will*'s the following Day,
Lie Snug, to hear what Cricks say.
And if you find the general Vogue
Pronounces you a stupid Rogue;
Damns all your Thoughts as low and little,
Sit still, and swallow down your Spittle.
Be silent as a Politician,
For talking may beget Suspicion:
Or praise the Judgment of the Town,
And help yourself to run it down.
Give up your fond paternal Pride,
Nor argue on the weaker Side;
For Poems read without a Name
We justly praise, or justly blame:
And Criticks have no partial Views,
Except they know whom they abuse.
And since you ne'er provok'd their Spight,
Depend upon't their Judgment's right:
But if you blab, you are undone;

Consider what a Risk you run.
You lose your Credit all at once;
The Town will mark you for a Dunce:
The vilest Doggrel *Grubstreet* sends,
Will pass for yours with Foes and Friends.
And you must bear the whole Disgrace,
'Till some fresh Blockhead takes your Place.

    Your Secret kept, your Poem sunk,
And sent in Quires to line a Trunk;
If still you be dispos'd to rhime,
Go try your Hand a second Time.
Again you fail, yet Safe's the Word,
Take Courage, and attempt a Third.
But first with Care imploy your Thoughts,
Where Criticks mark'd your former Faults.
The trivial Turns, the borrow'd Wit,
The *Similes* that nothing fit;
The *Cant* which ev'ry Fool repeats,
Town-Jests, and Coffee-house Conceits;
Descriptions tedious, flat and dry,
And introduc'd the Lord knows why;
Or where we find your Fury set
Against the harmless Alphabet;
On A's and B's your Malice vent,
While Readers wonder whom you meant.
A publick, or a private *Robber*;
A *Statesman*, or a South-Sea *Jobber*.
A *Prelate* who no God believes;
A Parliament, or Den of Thieves.
A Pick-purse, at the Bar, or Bench;
A Duchess, or a Suburb-Wench.
Or oft when Epithets you link,
In gaping Lines to fill a Chink;
Like stepping Stones to save a Stride,
In Streets where Kennels are too wide:

Or like a Heel-piece to support
A Cripple with one Foot too short:
Or like a Bridge that joins a Marish
To Moorlands of a diff'rent Parish.
So have I seen ill-coupled Hounds,
Drag diff'rent Ways in miry Grounds.
So Geographers in *Afric*-Maps
With Savage-Pictures fill their Gaps;
And o'er unhabitable Downs
Place Elephants for want of Towns. [. . .]

    Hobbes clearly proves that ev'ry Creature
Lives in a State of War by Nature.
The Greater for the Smaller watch,
But meddle seldom with their Match.
A Whale of moderate Size will draw
A Shole of Herrings down his Maw.
A Fox with Geese his Belly crams;
A Wolf destroys a thousand Lambs.
But search among the rhiming Race,
The Brave are worried by the Base.
If, on *Parnassus*' Top you sit,
You rarely bite, are always bit:
Each Poet of inferior Size
On you shall rail and criticize;
And strive to tear you Limb from Limb,
While others do as much for him.
The Vermin only teaze and pinch
Their Foes superior by an Inch.
So, Nat'ralists observe, a Flea
Hath smaller Fleas that on him prey,
And these have smaller yet to bite 'em,
And so proceed *ad infinitum*:
Thus ev'ry Poet in his Kind,
Is bit by him that comes behind;
Who, tho' too little to be seen,

Can teaze, and gall, and give the Spleen;
Call Dunces, Fools, and Sons of Whores,
Lay *Grubstreet* at each others Doors:
Extol the *Greek* and *Roman* Masters,
And curse our modern Poetasters.
Complain, as many an ancient Bard did,
How Genius is no more rewarded;
How wrong a Taste prevails among us;
How much our Ancestors out-sung us;
Can personate an awkward Scorn
For those who are not Poets born:
And all their Brother Dunces lash,
Who crowd the Press with hourly Trash.

foundered, lame; *bulk*, shop-front; *dropped*, born; *wipe*, swipe; *smokes*,
recognizes; *quit the cost*, break even; *in quires*, unbound; *kennels*, gutters;
marish, marsh; *personate*, simulate.

The Hardship put upon Ladies
Written in the Year 1733

Poor Ladies! though their Bus'ness be to play,
'Tis hard they must be busy Night and Day:
Why should they want the Privilege of Men,
And take some small Diversions now and then?
Had Women been the Makers of our Laws;
(And why they were not, I can see no Cause;)
The Men should slave at Cards from Morn to Night;
And Female Pleasures be to read and write.

On his own Deafness

Verticosus, inops, surdus, male gratus amicis;
Non campana sonans, tonitru non ab Jove missum,
Quod mage mirandum, saltem si credere fas est,
Non clamosa meas mulier jam percutit aures.

Deaf, giddy, helpless, left alone,
To all my Friends a Burthen grown,
No more I hear my Church's Bell,
Than if it rang out for my Knell:
At Thunder now no more I start,
Than at the Rumbling of a Cart:
Nay, what's incredible, alack!
I hardly hear a Woman's Clack.

On a Printer's being sent to Newgate

Better we all were in our Graves
Than live in Slavery to Slaves,
Worse than the Anarchy at Sea,
Where Fishes on each other prey;
Where ev'ry Trout can make as high Rants
O'er his Inferiors as our Tyrants;
And swagger while the Coast is clear:
But should a lordly Pike appear,
Away you see the Varlet scud,
Or hide his coward Snout in Mud.
Thus, if a Gudgeon meet a Roach
He dare not venture to approach;
Yet still has Impudence to rise,
And, like *Domitian*, leap at Flyes.

To Mrs Houghton of Bormount,
upon praising her Husband to Dr Swift

You always are making a God of your Spouse,
But this neither Reason nor Conscience allows;
Perhaps you will say, 'tis in Gratitude due,
And you adore him, because he adores you.
Your Argument's weak, and so you will find,
For you, by this Rule, must adore all Mankind.

An Epigram on Scolding

Great Folks are of a finer Mold;
Lord! how politely they can scold;
While a coarse *English* Tongue will itch,
For Whore and Rogue; and Dog and Bitch.

Verses made for Women who cry Apples, etc.

APPLES

Come buy my fine Wares,
Plumbs, Apples and Pears,
A hundred a Penny,
In Conscience too many,
Come, will you have any;
My Children are seven,
I wish them in Heaven,
My Husband's a Sot,
With his Pipe and his Pot,
Not a Farthing will gain 'em,
And I must maintain 'em.

ASPARAGUS

Ripe 'Sparagrass,
Fit for Lad or Lass,
To make their Water pass:
   O, 'tis pretty Picking
   With a tender Chicken.

ONYONS

Come, follow me by the Smell,
Here's delicate Onyons to sell,
I promise to use you well.
They make the Blood warmer,
You'll feed like a Farmer:
For this is ev'ry Cook's Opinion,
No sav'ry Dish without an Onyon;
But lest your Kissing should be spoyl'd,
Your Onyons must be th'roughly boyl'd;
     Or else you may spare

Your Mistress a Share,
The Secret will never be known;
    She cannot discover
    The Breath of her Lover,
But think it as sweet as her own.

OYSTERS

Charming Oysters I cry,
My Masters come buy,
So plump and so fresh,
So sweet is their Flesh,
No *Colchester* Oyster,
Is sweeter and moyster,
Your Stomach they settle,
And rouse up your Mettle,
They'll make you a Dad
Of a Lass or a Lad;
And, Madam your Wife
They'll please to the Life;
Be she barren, be she old,
Be she Slut, or be she Scold,
Eat my Oysters, and lye near her,
She'll be fruitful, never fear her.

HERRINGS

Be not sparing,
Leave off swearing
Buy my Herring
Fresh from *Malahide*,
Better ne'er was try'd.
Come eat 'em with pure fresh Butter and Mustard,
Their Bellies are soft, and as white as a Custard.
Come, Six-pence a Dozen to get me some Bread,
Or, like my own Herrings, I soon shall be dead.

ORANGES

Come, buy my fine Oranges, Sauce for your Veal,
And charming when squeez'd in a Pot of brown Ale.
Well roasted, with Sugar and Wine in a Cup,
They'll make a sweet Bishop when Gentlefolks sup.

bishop, a hot punch

A Cantata

[Musical setting by John Echlin, 1746]

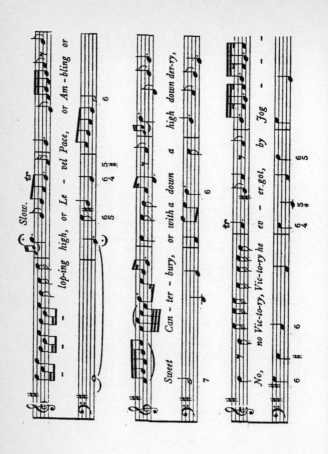

115

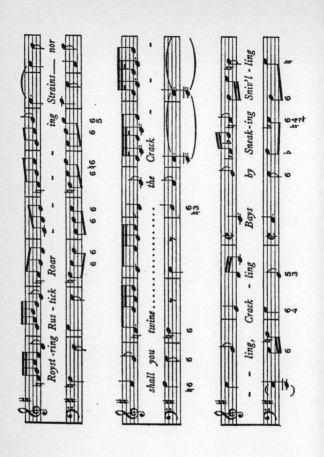

117

119